THE FEATURED DRUMMER

by Terry Silverlight

Amsco Publications
A Part of **The Music Sales Group**
New York/London/Paris/Sydney/Copenhagen/Berlin/Tokyo/Madrid

Project Editor: Felipe Orozco
Graphic Design: Sol & Luna Creations

Copyright © 2005 Amsco Publications
A Division of Music Sales Corporation, New York

Order No. AM 980232
US International Standard Book Number: 0.8256.2977.2
UK International Standard Book Number: 1.84449.541.8

Exclusive Distributors:
Music Sales Corporation
257 Park Avenue South, New York, NY. 10010 USA
Music Sales Limited
8/9 Frith Street, London W1D 3JB England
Music Sales Pty. Limited
120 Rothschild Street, Rosebery, Sydney, NSW 2018, Australia

Printed in the United States of America
by Vicks Lithograph and Printing Corporation

Table of Contents

CD Tracks

Practice CD

1. Shuffle – Groove 1
2. Shuffle – Groove 2
3. Shuffle – Groove 3
4. Shuffle – Groove 4
5. Shuffle groups of 3s – Fill 1, Fill 2, Fill 3
6. Shuffle groups of 3s – Fill 4, Fill 5, Fill 6
7. Shuffle groups of 3s – Fill 7, Fill 8, Fill 9
8. Shuffle groups of 3s – Fill 10, Fill 11
9. Shuffle groups of 4s – Fill 1, Fill 2, Fill 3
10. Shuffle groups of 4s – Fill 4, Fill 5, Fill 6
11. Shuffle groups of 4s – Fill 7, Fill 8, Fill 9
12. Shuffle groups of 4s – Fill 10, Fill 11
13. Shuffle groups of 5s – Fill 1, Fill 2, Fill 3
14. Shuffle groups of 5s – Fill 4, Fill 5, Fill 6
15. Shuffle groups of 5s – Fill 7, Fill 8, Fill 9
16. Shuffle groups of 5s – Fill 10, Fill 11
17. Shuffle groups of 7s – Fill 1, Fill 2, Fill 3
18. Shuffle groups of 7s – Fill 4, Fill 5, Fill 6
19. Shuffle groups of 7s – Fill 7, Fill 8, Fill 9
20. Shuffle groups of 7s – Fill 10, Fill 11
21. Samba – Groove 1
22. Samba – Groove 2
23. Samba – Groove 3
24. Samba – Groove 4
25. Samba groups of 3s – Fill 1, Fill 2, Fill 3
26. Samba groups of 3s – Fill 4, Fill 5, Fill 6
27. Samba groups of 3s – Fill 7, Fill 8, Fill 9
28. Samba groups of 3s – Fill 10, Fill 11
29. Samba groups of 4s – Fill 1, Fill 2, Fill 3
30. Samba groups of 4s – Fill 4, Fill 5, Fill 6
31. Samba groups of 4s – Fill 7, Fill 8, Fill 9
32. Samba groups of 4s – Fill 10, Fill 11
33. Samba groups of 5s – Fill 1, Fill 2, Fill 3
34. Samba groups of 5s – Fill 4, Fill 5, Fill 6
35. Samba groups of 5s – Fill 7, Fill 8, Fill 9
36. Samba groups of 5s – Fill 10, Fill 11
37. Samba groups of 7s – Fill 1, Fill 2, Fill 3
38. Samba groups of 7s – Fill 4, Fill 5, Fill 6
39. Samba groups of 7s – Fill 7, Fill 8, Fill 9
40. Samba groups of 7s – Fill 10, Fill 11
41. Six-Eight – Groove 1
42. Six-Eight – Groove 2
43. Six-Eight – Groove 3
44. Six-Eight – Groove 4
45. Six-Eight groups of 3s – Fill 1, Fill 2, Fill 3
46. Six-Eight groups of 3s – Fill 4, Fill 5, Fill 6
47. Six-Eight groups of 3s – Fill 7, Fill 8, Fill 9
48. Six-Eight groups of 3s – Fill 10, Fill 11
49. Six-Eight groups of 4s – Fill 1, Fill 2, Fill 3
50. Six-Eight groups of 4s – Fill 4, Fill 5, Fill 6
51. Six-Eight groups of 4s – Fill 7, Fill 8, Fill 9
52. Six-Eight groups of 4s – Fill 10, Fill 11
53. Six-Eight groups of 5s – Fill 1, Fill 2, Fill 3
54. Six-Eight groups of 5s – Fill 4, Fill 5, Fill 6
55. Six-Eight groups of 5s – Fill 7, Fill 8, Fill 9
56. Six-Eight groups of 5s – Fill 10, Fill 11
57. Six-Eight groups of 7s – Fill 1, Fill 2, Fill 3
58. Six-Eight groups of 7s – Fill 4, Fill 5, Fill 6
59. Six-Eight groups of 7s – Fill 7, Fill 8, Fill 9
60. Six-Eight groups of 7s – Fill 10, Fill 11
61. Funk – Groove 1
62. Funk – Groove 2
63. Funk – Groove 3
64. Funk – Groove 4
65. Funk groups of 3s – Fill 1, Fill 2, Fill 3
66. Funk groups of 3s – Fill 4, Fill 5, Fill 6
67. Funk groups of 3s – Fill 7, Fill 8, Fill 9
68. Funk groups of 3s – Fill 10, Fill 11
69. Funk groups of 4s – Fill 1, Fill 2, Fill 3
70. Funk groups of 4s – Fill 4, Fill 5, Fill 6
71. Funk groups of 4s – Fill 7, Fill 8, Fill 9
72. Funk groups of 4s – Fill 10, Fill 11
73. Funk groups of 5s – Fill 1, Fill 2, Fill 3
74. Funk groups of 5s – Fill 4, Fill 5, Fill 6
75. Funk groups of 5s – Fill 7, Fill 8, Fill 9
76. Funk groups of 5s – Fill 10, Fill 11
77. Funk groups of 7s – Fill 1, Fill 2, Fill 3
78. Funk groups of 7s – Fill 4, Fill 5, Fill 6
79. Funk groups of 7s – Fill 7, Fill 8, Fill 9
80. Funk groups of 7s – Fill 10, Fill 11

Performance CD

1. Shuffle song
2. Samba song
3. Six–Eight song
4. Funk song
5. Phantom of Bebopera*
6. Pugnacious*

from Terry Silverlight's CD, "Wild." Used by Permission.

Introduction

The exercises in this book were developed from live playing situations. When I was the drummer in the band Barry Miles and Silverlight, the musical environment gave me the opportunity to play unconventional figures not only in my solos, but behind all the other great soloists in the band as well. The rhythmic ideas and patterns flowed from me and I began to see a new concept take shape.

My overall vision was to play figures over the barline, mostly in groupings of three, four, five, and seven notes, usually over the course of two, four, or eight bars. Accenting the first note of each group, experimenting with different stickings, and orchestrating the groupings in various ways around the drumset created a very unique sound and gave the music color, shape, and dynamics.

I decided to write down a few patterns, and soon discovered that there were endless variations that could be created from the core concept. This led me to systematically arrange eleven of these patterns in each grouping as both hands–only and four–way coordination exercises, hence the birth of *The Featured Drummer*. I've continued to develop this concept and work it into my playing whenever the occasion is appropriate.

In this new version of the book, I thought it would be important to include an audio CD of all the exercises in a musical setting. The intent is to show how I was originally inspired to create them from the spirit of the music itself. I am fortunate to have two all–time great musicians play along with me who truly have an understanding and feel for the book's concept: Barry Miles and John Patitucci. Although this book was arranged specifically for the drumset, the content crosses over and can be applied to any instrument.

I encourage the readers to not only work hard and learn the challenging patterns contained herein, but to create their own original variations and incorporate them into their playing. Enjoy!

–Terry Silverlight

Foreword

The second half of the twentieth century saw a revolution in contemporary drumming styles and techniques. Jazz drumming was greatly affected by the influence of rock, the complex polyrhythms of Indian *tabla* playing, and the intricate syncopations of Brazilian samba music. Drummers like Tony Williams, Billy Cobham, and Terry Silverlight were some of the very first to incorporate these styles and techniques into jazz, helping to pave the way for a fusion of musical styles.

With any new style of music, it always takes a while before a book comes along that presents a practical method for a student to learn the techniques of that style. *The Featured Drummer* will take the serious student to the core of jazz–fusion in a straightforward and organized manner.

Mr. Silverlight has mapped out a plan of exercises to guide the student into the mastery of his concept. At the same time, the exercises are flexible enough to be modified for practical use when playing in a live situation. I must warn the student who begins approaching the exercises in this book that its mastery is no easy task. I believe that what the author has written will open many doors to the drummer who is seriously trying to absorb these new techniques. Although there is no substitute for hard work, this book will give that work a positive direction.

For those students who are prepared to meet the challenge that this book offers, they will be provided with invaluable insights and exercises that will help them gain proficiency in contemporary drumming.

–Barry Miles
(composer, author, performer, bandleader, arranger, recording artist)

Instructions

Drumset Key

The following key explains the drums to be played. The top cymbal line can be dedicated to one cymbal or can be freely orchestrated with a variety of cymbals, as is demonstrated on the audio CD. The same applies to the tom line, which may be assigned to just one tom or freely orchestrated with various toms.

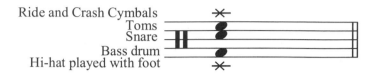

*Except *shuffle groove* 4 and *funk grooves* 3 and 4, where the hi–hat line is played with the right hand (x= closed, o= open)

Hands only warm–up exercises

Each chapter begins with *hands only warm–up exercises*. These are to be played on a practice pad or snare drum. Observe stickings and accent markings carefully.

Some of the exercises have both **R** and **L** sticking marks. This means that at this particular spot both hands play simultaneously. Try switching the stickings so that you can practice ambidextrously.

Initially, you should follow this key with traditional right- or left-handed stickings. Once this is mastered, it is encouraged to create alternate stickings for the purposes of variety and coordination.

Songs

After the *hands only warm–up exercises* there is a song for each of the chapter styles. John Patitucci, Barry Miles and myself (Terry Silverlight) have recorded these songs on the Performance CD, Check them out!

Grooves and fills

The different grooves and fills played in each song are presented individually in music notation. There are four grooves and eleven fills within each of the four segments in each chapter (*Threes, Fours, Fives, and Sevens*).

Both the grooves and the fills have a timing mark on the top left side of the notation. This is the elapsed time where each groove or fill can be found on the live–performance CD. They have also been recorded individually at a moderate tempo on the practice CD.

Each four–bar groove is written as two bars with a repeat sign, so be sure to play the two bars twice, making the groove a total of four bars.

How to study each chapter

This guide will lead you step by step through chapter one. Apply the same steps for each chapter.

Step one

Without a click, examine *Chapter 1: Groove 1* note–by–note, limb–by–limb, and become familiar with which notes are played simultaneously and which are not.

Step two

Set up a metronome click to ♩=20 bpm and try to play the groove in time with the click. Pay close attention to the accent markings.

Step three

Once a steady, smooth, and comfortable feel has been established at this speed, increase the tempo gradually by 5–10 bpm. Don't move to a faster tempo until the previous one has become completely comfortable. Jumping too quickly to achieve speed without precision will bring sloppy, uneven results.

Step four

Without a click, play the six notes enclosed in the box that appears at the beginning of *Fill 1*.

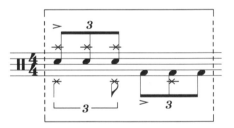

The boxes at the beginning of each fill throughout this book indicate the grouping used in that fill. *Fill 1* is a six–note grouping. Even though the first segment of this chapter is titled *Threes*, a six–note grouping falls into this category. (Six is a multiple of three, and some fills are more musical containing six notes rather than just three.) Therefore, some fills will have three–note groupings and some will have six–note groupings. The same holds for the *Fours* segment, where some fills will be four–note groupings and some will be eight–note groupings. The segment *Fives* will contain exercises with five–note groupings and ten–note groupings, and the segment *Sevens* will contain exercises with seven–note groupings and fourteen–note groupings.

Step five

Set up a metronome click to ♩=20 bpm. Try to play the six notes in the box in time to the click.

Step six

Once that is mastered, continue playing in time to the click for the remainder of the exercise.

Each of the exercises in this book has a length of four bars. However, note that it would take three bars for each grouping of *Threes* to complete a cycle (so that the beginning of the grouping lands back on beat one). It would take *Fours* four bars to complete a cycle (which is how they are written throughout the book). *Fives* would complete its cycle in five bars, and *Sevens* would cycle in seven bars. For the sake of musicality and continuity throughout this book, each exercise is limited to four bars. Therefore, with the exception of the *Fours* segments, the final grouping at the end of the fourth bar is cut short.

Step seven

Once a steady, smooth, comfortable feel has been established at this speed, increase the tempo gradually by 5–10 bpm. Again, do not move to a faster tempo until the previous one has become completely comfortable.

Step eight

Proceed to the next four–bar groove and begin practicing in the same manner as described above, then do the same with the fills. Continue this way until all grooves and fills have been mastered.

Step nine

Once all this has been achieved, play along with the live CD track, alternating grooves and fills.

Step ten

Proceed to chapters 2, 3, and 4 and practice in the same manner as suggested for chapter 1.

When first approaching the exercises in this book, it is important to count out loud to mark the basic pulse, especially at the beginning of each bar. Playing the exercises without knowing how they relate to the basic pulse defeats our purpose. Play to a click, count along with it, and pay close attention while coordinating the exercise. Do not move on to the next exercise until this is mastered. The objective is to hear these exercises in relation to the pulse. You must know exactly where each bar begins and where you are within that bar. By doing this, it will be easier to eventually count to yourself and ultimately just *feel* the exercises naturally against the basic pulse. It's a process that will take time, but cannot be achieved without following these steps.

Chapter 1: Shuffle

Four–bar shuffle grooves alternating with
four–bar eighth–note triplet exercises accented
in groups of threes, fours, fives, and sevens.

Hands Only: Eighth–note triplets accented in groups of three ♩= 140

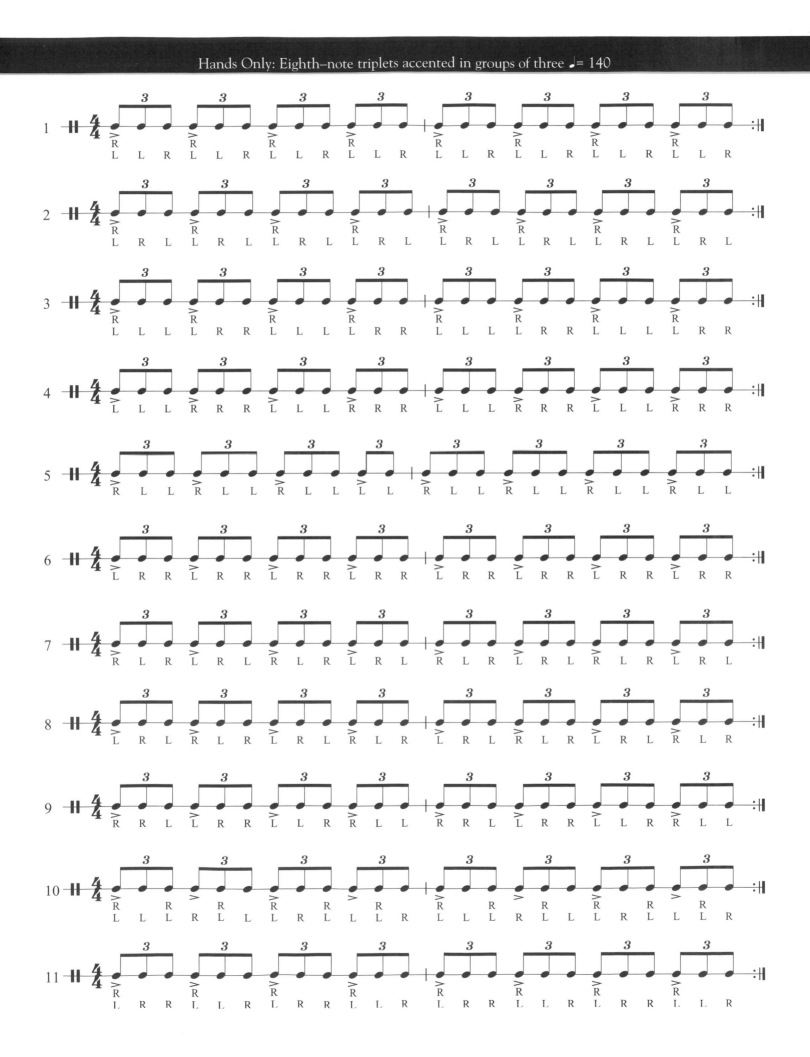

12

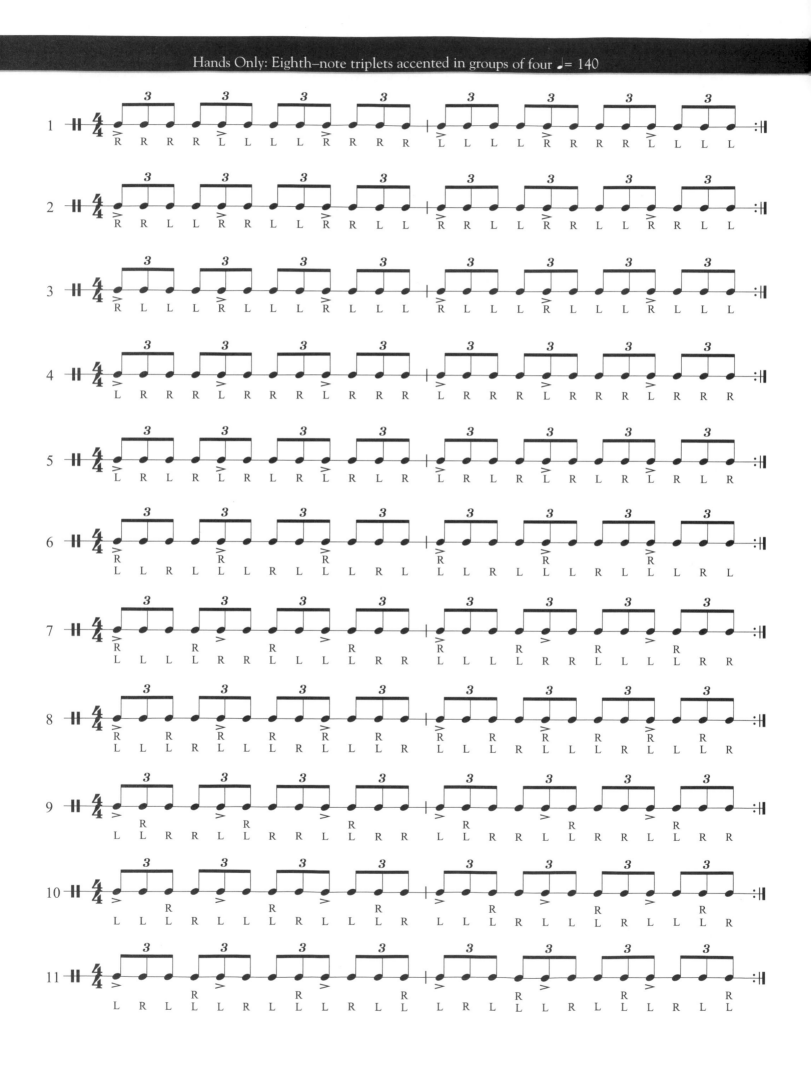

Hands Only: Eighth–note triplets accented in groups of five ♩= 140

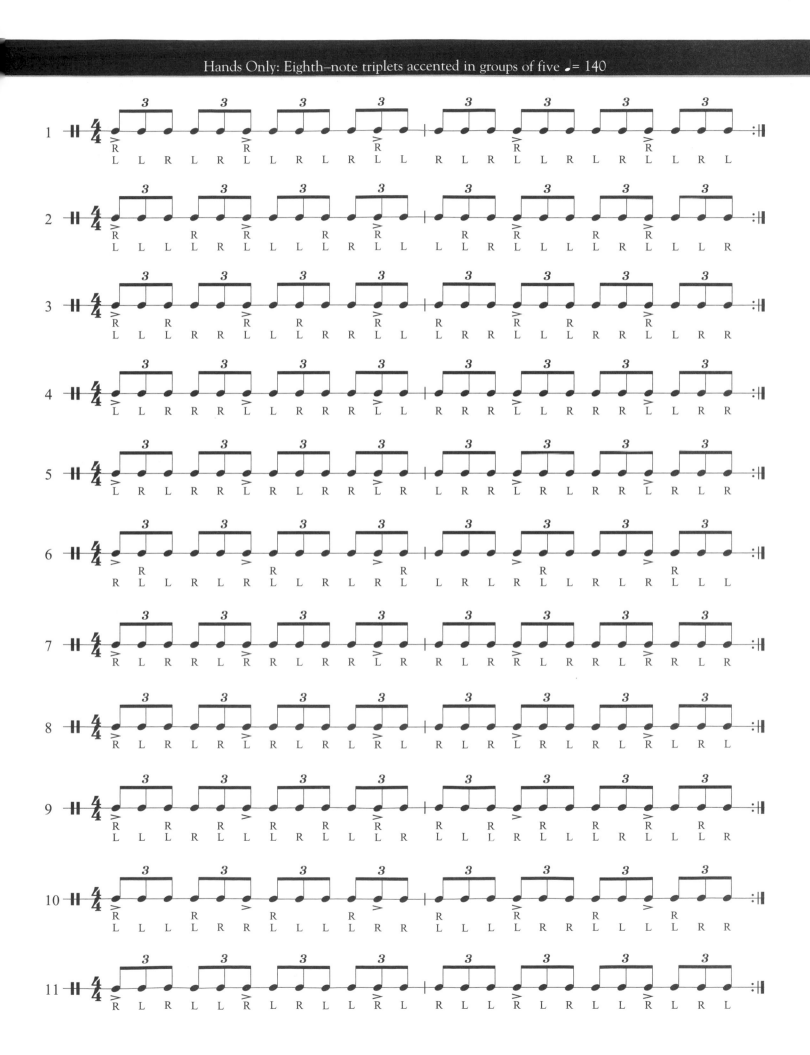

Hands Only: Eighth–note triplets accented in groups of seven ♩=140

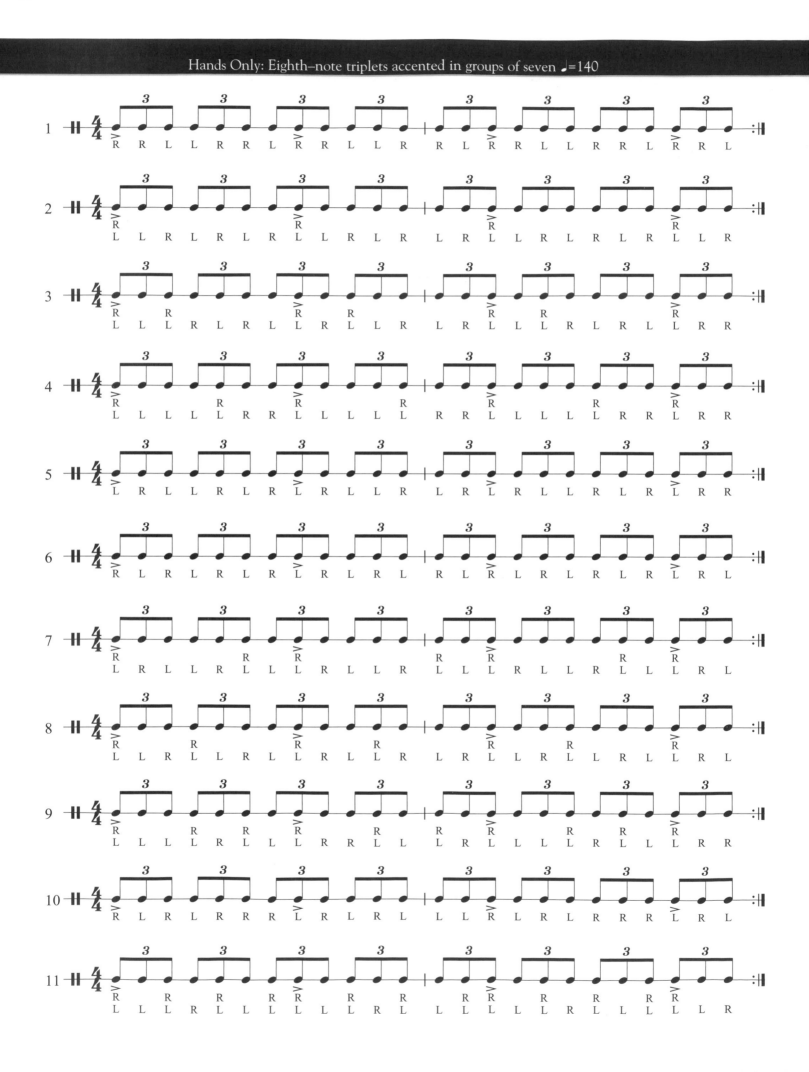

Shuffle Song

Grooves

Listen to the CD and notice how the accents are interpreted by using a variety of cymbals and toms instead of just one. The player can take liberties like this to enhance the musical phrasing and dynamics.

Regular rhythm

This is what a typical shuffle pattern looks like:

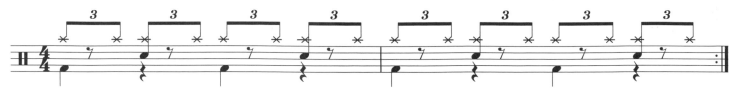

Now let's review the different variations.

Groove 1

Practice CD	Track 1	
Performance CD	Track 1	Time 0:43

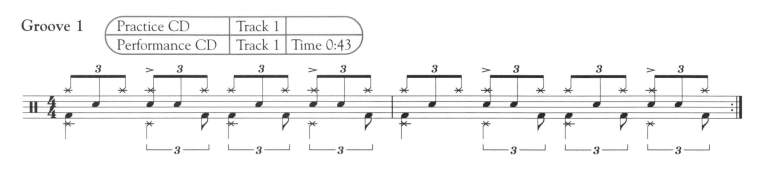

Groove 2

Practice CD	Track 2	
Performance CD	Track 1	Time 0:56

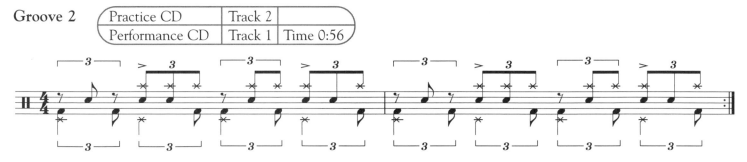

Groove 3

Practice CD	Track 3	
Performance CD	Track 1	Time 1:10

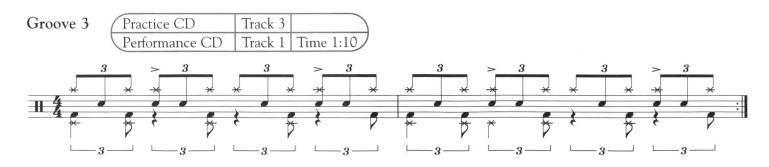

Groove 4

Practice CD	Track 4	
Performance CD	Track 1	Time 1:24

In this groove, the hi–hat pattern is played with the right hand, not the left foot as it is mostly played throughout the book.

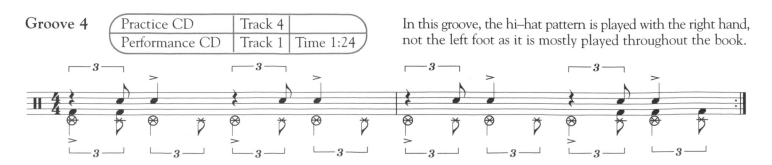

Fills

Groups of Threes

Fill 1

Practice CD	Track 5	
Performance CD	Track 1	Time 0:49

Fill 2

Practice CD	Track 5	
Performance CD	Track 1	Time 1:03

Fill 3

Practice CD	Track 5	
Performance CD	Track 1	Time 1:17

Fill 4

Practice CD	Track 6	
Performance CD	Track 1	Time 1:30

Fill 5

Practice CD	Track 6	
Performance CD	Track 1	Time 1:44

Check out *Fill 5* (CD track 6). Every six notes are emphasized instead of every three notes for phrasing purposes.

Fill 6

Practice CD	Track 6	
Performance CD	Track 1	Time 1:58

Pay attention to *Fill 6* (CD track 6). Notice how the bass drum is emphasized on every six notes instead of every three notes to change the color of the fill.

Fill 7

Practice CD	Track 7	
Performance CD	Track 1	Time 2:12

Fill 8

Practice CD	Track 7	
Performance CD	Track 1	Time 2:25

Fill 9

Practice CD	Track 7	
Performance CD	Track 1	Time 2:39

Fill 10

Practice CD	Track 8	
Performance CD	Track 1	Time 2:53

Fill 11

Practice CD	Track 8	
Performance CD	Track 1	Time 3:06

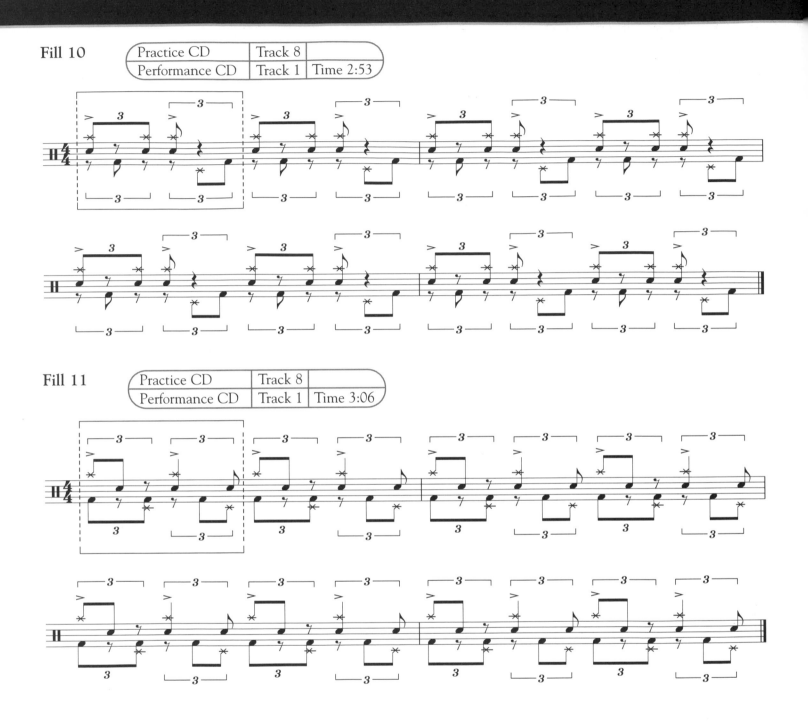

Groups of Fours

Fill 1

Practice CD	Track 9	
Performance CD	Track 1	Time 3:20

Listen to *Fill 3* (CD track 9). Every eight notes are emphasized instead of every four notes for phrasing purposes.

Fill 2

Practice CD	Track 9	
Performance CD	Track 1	Time 3:34

Fill 3

Practice CD	Track 9	
Performance CD	Track 1	Time 3:48

Fill 4

Practice CD	Track 10	
Performance CD	Track 1	Time 4:01

Fill 5

Practice CD	Track 10	
Performance CD	Track 1	Time 4:15

Fill 6

Practice CD	Track 10	
Performance CD	Track 1	Time 4:29

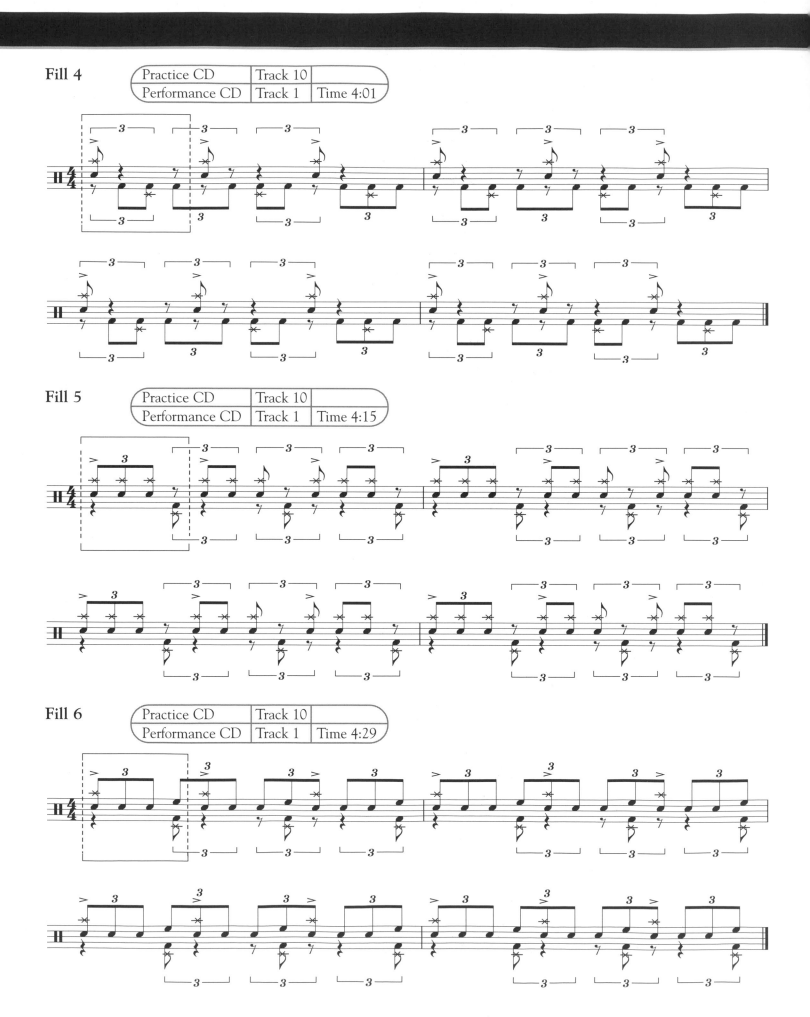

Fill 7

Practice CD	Track 11	
Performance CD	Track 1	Time 4:42

In *Fills* 8, 9, and 10 (tracks 11 and 12 of the practice CD), the crashes shift the accent of the four–note grouping beginning on the downbeat. Displacing the grouped accents like this adds variety and helps the examples sound more musical and less technical.

Try this approach with all the exercises throughout the book.

Fill 8

Practice CD	Track 11	
Performance CD	Track 1	Time 4:56

Fill 9

Practice CD	Track 11	
Performance CD	Track 1	Time 5:10

Fill 10

Practice CD	Track 12	
Performance CD	Track 1	Time 5:24

Fill 11

Practice CD	Track 12	
Performance CD	Track 1	Time 5:37

Groups of Fives

Fill 1

Practice CD	Track 13	
Performance CD	Track 1	Time 5:51

Fill 1 on track 13 of the practice CD emphasizes every ten notes instead of every five notes for phrasing purposes.

Fill 2

Practice CD	Track 13	
Performance CD	Track 1	Time 6:04

Fill 3

Practice CD	Track 13	
Performance CD	Track 1	Time 6:18

26

Fill 7

Practice CD	Track 15	
Performance CD	Track 1	Time 7:13

Fill 8

Practice CD	Track 15	
Performance CD	Track 1	Time 7:27

Fill 9

Practice CD	Track 15	
Performance CD	Track 1	Time 7:41

Fill 10

Practice CD	Track 16	
Performance CD	Track 1	Time 7:54

Fill 11

Practice CD	Track 16	
Performance CD	Track 1	Time 8:08

Groups of Sevens

Fill 1

Practice CD	Track 17	
Performance CD	Track 1	Time 8:22

Fill 2

Practice CD	Track 17	
Performance CD	Track 1	Time 8:36

Fill 3

Practice CD	Track 17	
Performance CD	Track 1	Time 8:49

Fill 4

Practice CD	Track 18	
Performance CD	Track 1	Time 9:03

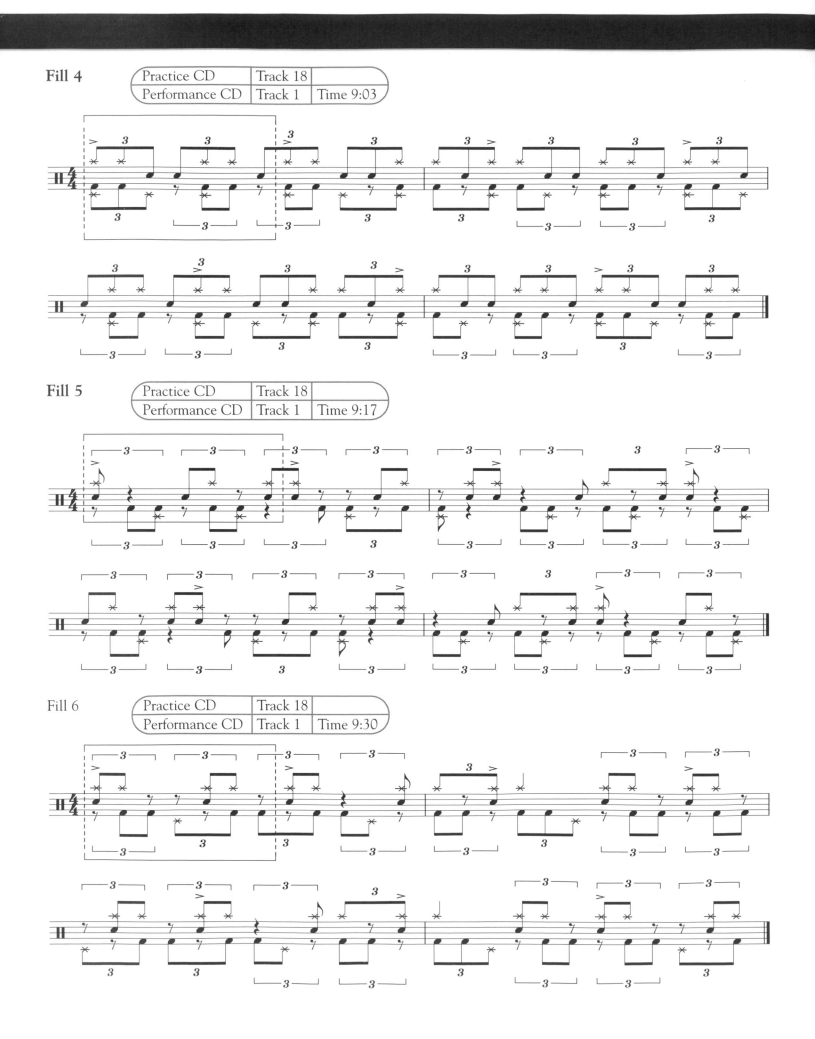

Fill 5

Practice CD	Track 18	
Performance CD	Track 1	Time 9:17

Fill 6

Practice CD	Track 18	
Performance CD	Track 1	Time 9:30

Fill 7

| Practice CD | Track 19 | |
| Performance CD | Track 1 | Time 9:44 |

Fill 8

| Practice CD | Track 19 | |
| Performance CD | Track 1 | Time 9:58 |

Fill 9

| Practice CD | Track 19 | |
| Performance CD | Track 1 | Time 10:11 |

Fill 10

Practice CD	Track 20	
Performance CD	Track 1	Time 10:25

Fill 11

Practice CD	Track 20	
Performance CD	Track 1	Time 10:39

Chapter 2: Samba

Four–bar samba grooves alternating with
four–bar sixteenth–note exercises accented in
groups of threes, fours, fives, and sevens.

Hands Only: Sixteenth notes accented in groups of three ♩= 130

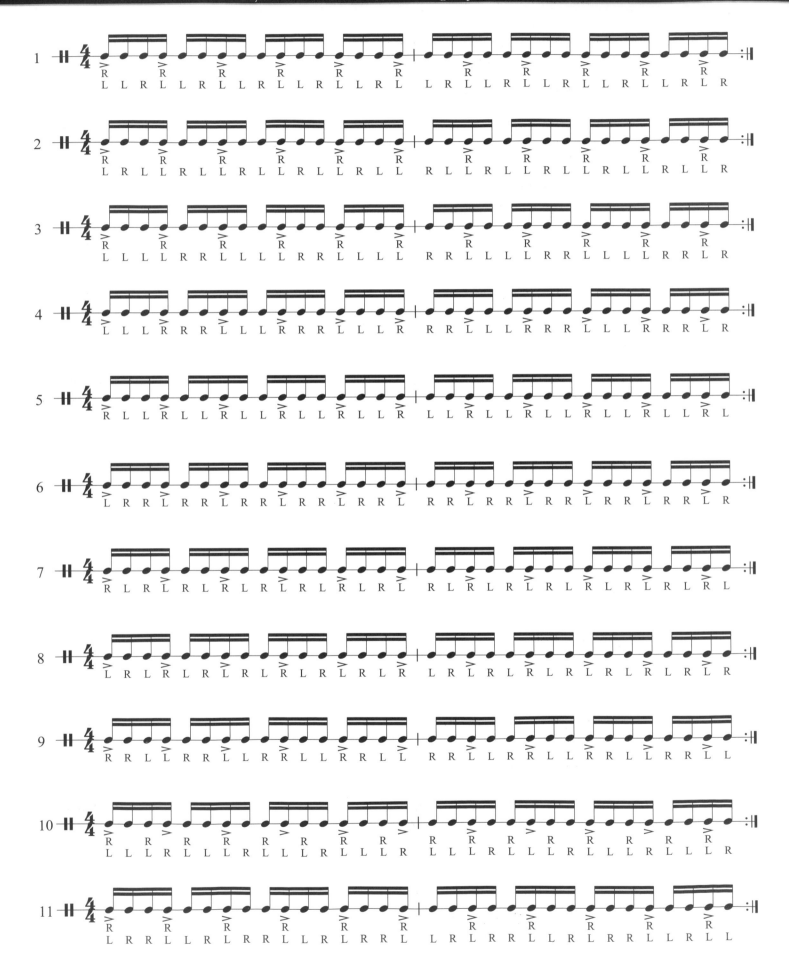

Hands Only: Sixteenth notes accented in groups of four ♩= 130

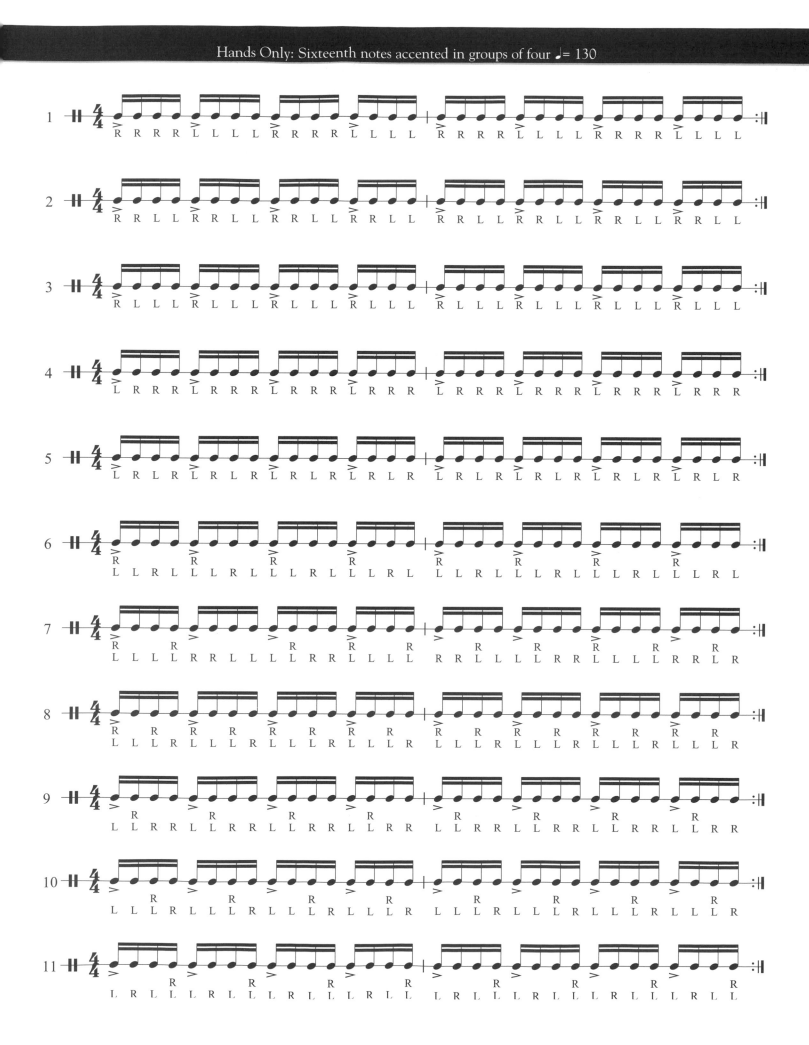

Hands Only: Sixteenth notes accented in groups of five ♩= 130

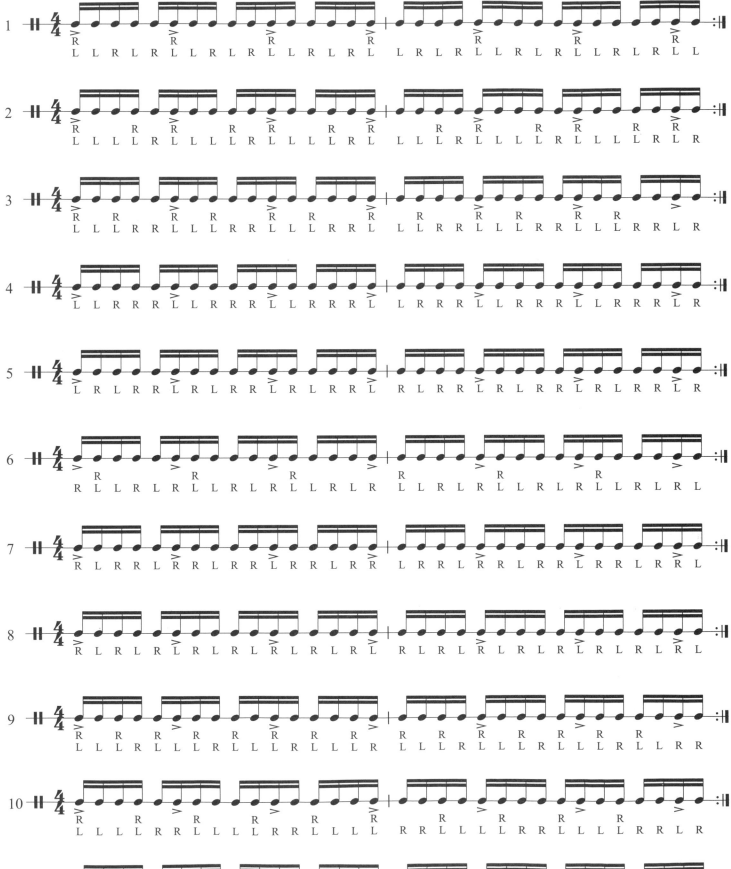

Hands Only: Sixteenth notes accented in groups of seven ♩= 130

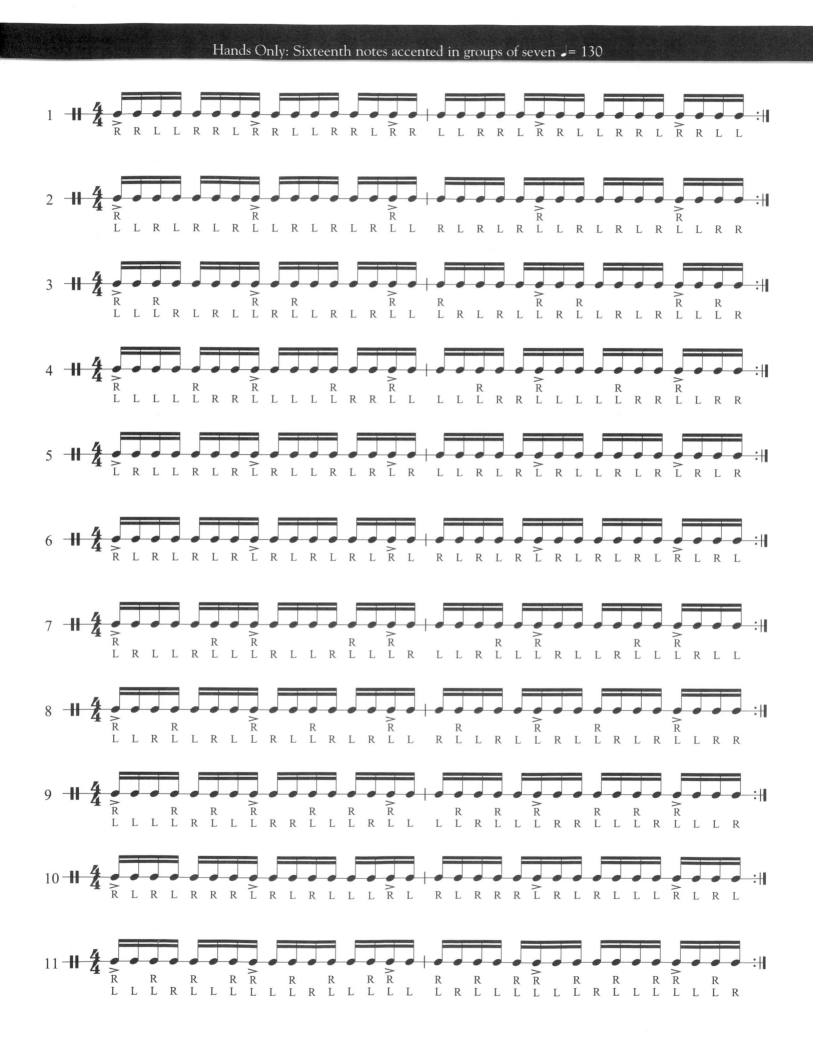

Samba Song

Fine

Grooves

Regular rhythm

This is what a typical samba pattern looks like:

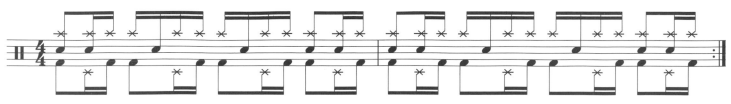

Now let's review different variations.
Putting more emphasis on selected accents and less on others creates dynamics, color, and phrasing.

Groove 1

Practice CD	Track 21	
Performance CD	Track 2	Time 0:37

Groove 2

Practice CD	Track 22	
Performance CD	Track 2	Time 0:52

Groove 3

Practice CD	Track 23	
Performance CD	Track 2	Time 1:07

Groove 4

Practice CD	Track 24	
Performance CD	Track 2	Time 1:22

Fills

Groups of Threes

Fill 1

Practice CD	Track 25	
Performance CD	Track 2	Time 0:45

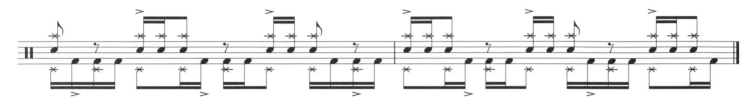

Fill 2

Practice CD	Track 25	
Performance CD	Track 2	Time 1:00

Fill 3

Practice CD	Track 25	
Performance CD	Track 1	Time 1:14

Fill 4

Practice CD	Track 26	
Performance CD	Track 1	Time 1:29

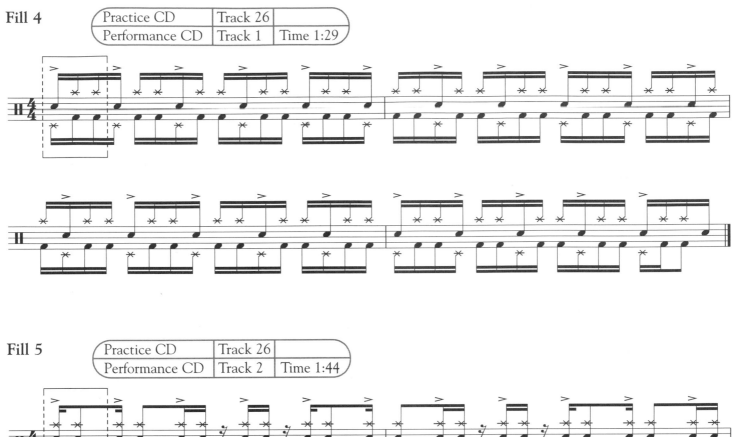

Fill 5

Practice CD	Track 26	
Performance CD	Track 2	Time 1:44

Fill 6

Practice CD	Track 26	
Performance CD	Track 1	Time 1:59

Notice that *Fills 7* and *10* (CD tracks 27 and 28) emphasize the patterns every six notes instead of every three notes. This is done to create a different color in the music. Other patterns of *Threes* can be approached this way too.

Fill 7

Practice CD	Track 27	
Performance CD	Track 2	Time 2:13

Fill 8

Practice CD	Track 27	
Performance CD	Track 2	Time 2:28

Fill 9

Practice CD	Track 27	
Performance CD	Track 2	Time 2:43

Fill 10

Practice CD	Track 28	
Performance CD	Track 2	Time 2:58

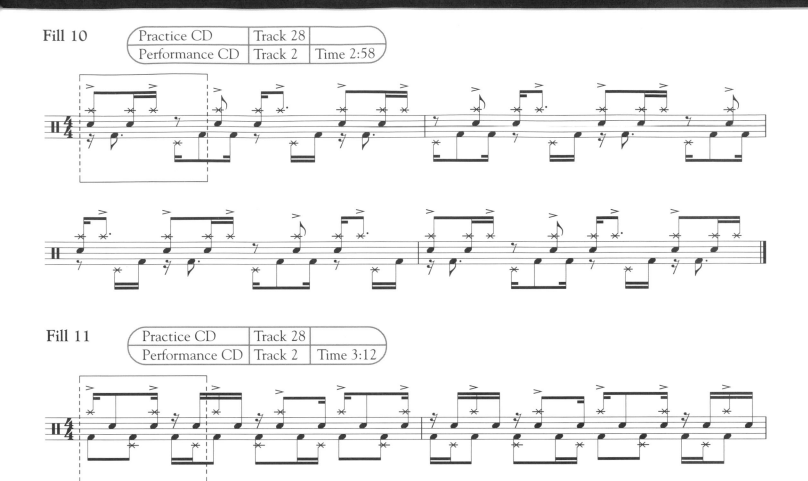

Fill 11

Practice CD	Track 28	
Performance CD	Track 2	Time 3:12

Groups of Fours

Notice on the audio CD how this section emphasizes every eight notes instead of every four notes.

Fill 1

Practice CD	Track 29	
Performance CD	Track 2	Time 3:27

Fill 2

Practice CD	Track 29	
Performance CD	Track 2	Time 3:42

Fill 3

Practice CD	Track 29	
Performance CD	Track 2	Time 3:57

Fill 4

Practice CD	Track 30	
Performance CD	Track 2	Time 4:12

Fill 5

Practice CD	Track 30	
Performance CD	Track 2	Time 4:27

Fill 6

Practice CD	Track 30	
Performance CD	Track 2	Time 4:41

Fill 7

Practice CD	Track 31	
Performance CD	Track 2	Time 4:56

In Fill 7 (Practice CD Track 31), notice the emphasis on the "ands" (where the crashes fall) instead of on the downbeats. This adds color to the music. On the audio examples throughout this section, the emphasis tends to fall on the offbeat crashes instead of on the downbeats.

Fill 8

Practice CD	Track 31	
Performance CD	Track 2	Time 5:11

Fill 9

Practice CD	Track 31	
Performance CD	Track 2	Time 5:25

Fill 10

| Practice CD | Track 32 | |
| Performance CD | Track 2 | Time 5:40 |

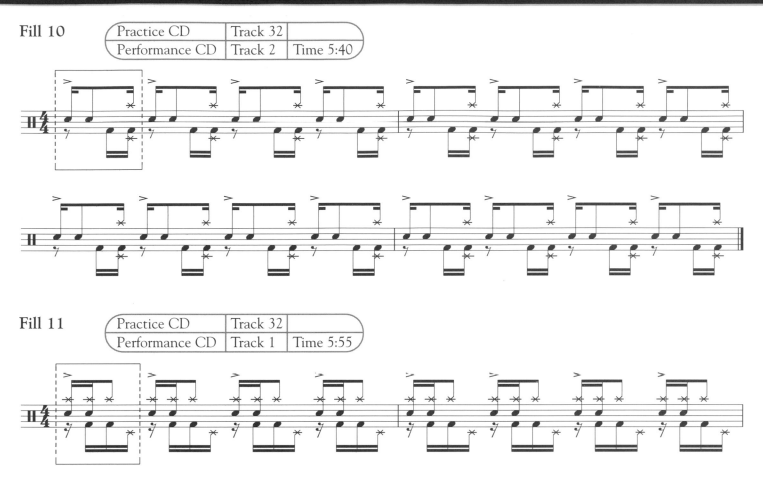

Fill 11

| Practice CD | Track 32 | |
| Performance CD | Track 1 | Time 5:55 |

Groups of Fives

Fill 1

Practice CD	Track 33	
Performance CD	Track 2	Time 6:10

Check track 33 on the practice CD. The accents fall on the offbeat crashes instead of on the downbeat of each five–note grouping as written. Displacing the grouped accents like this adds variety. Try this approach with all the exercises throughout the book.

Fill 2

Practice CD	Track 33	
Performance CD	Track 2	Time 6:24

Fill 3

Practice CD	Track 33	
Performance CD	Track 2	Time 6:39

Fill 4

Practice CD	Track 34	
Performance CD	Track 2	Time 6:54

Fill 5

Practice CD	Track 34	
Performance CD	Track 2	Time 7:09

Fill 6

Practice CD	Track 34	
Performance CD	Track 2	Time 7:24

Fill 7

| Practice CD | Track 35 | |
| Performance CD | Track 2 | Time 7:38 |

Fill 8

| Practice CD | Track 35 | |
| Performance CD | Track 2 | Time 7:53 |

Fill 9

| Practice CD | Track 35 | |
| Performance CD | Track 2 | Time 8:08 |

Fill 10

| Practice CD | Track 36 | |
| Performance CD | Track 2 | Time 8:23 |

Fill 11

| Practice CD | Track 36 | |
| Performance CD | Track 2 | Time 8:37 |

Groups of Sevens

Fill 1

Practice CD	Track 37	
Performance CD	Track 2	Time 8:52

Fill 2

Practice CD	Track 37	
Performance CD	Track 2	Time 9:07

Fill 3

Practice CD	Track 37	
Performance CD	Track 2	Time 9:22

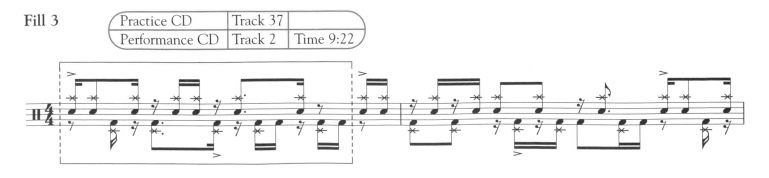

Fill 4

Practice CD	Track 38	
Performance CD	Track 2	Time 9:36

Fill 5

Practice CD	Track 38	
Performance CD	Track 2	Time 9:51

Fill 6

Practice CD	Track 38	
Performance CD	Track 2	Time 10:06

Fill 7

Practice CD	Track 39	
Performance CD	Track 2	Time 10:21

Fill 8

Practice CD	Track 39	
Performance CD	Track 2	Time 10:35

Fill 9

Practice CD	Track 39	
Performance CD	Track 2	Time 10:50

Fill 10

Practice CD	Track 40	
Performance CD	Track 2	Time 11:05

Fill 11

Practice CD	Track 40	
Performance CD	Track 2	Time 11:20

Chapter 3: Six-Eight

Four-bar six-eight grooves alternating with
four-bar sixteenth note exercises accented in
groups of threes, fours, fives, and sevens.

Hands Only: Sixteenth notes accented in groups of three ♪ = 215

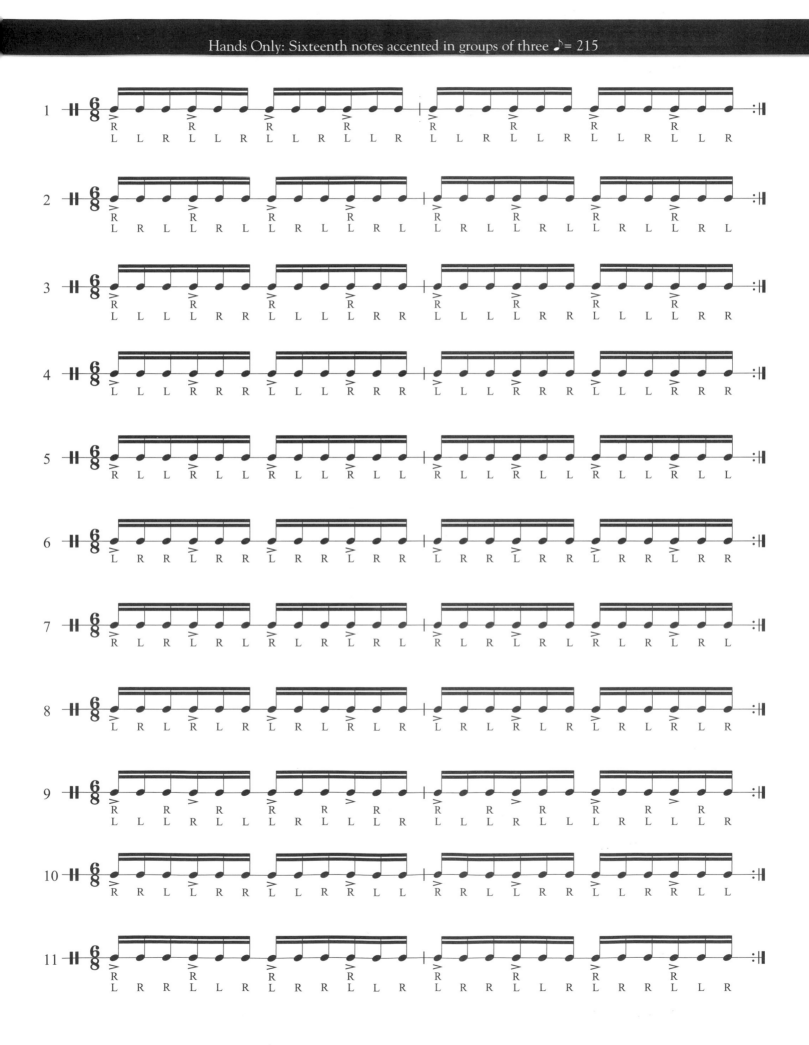

Hands Only: Sixteenth notes accented in groups of four ♪= 215

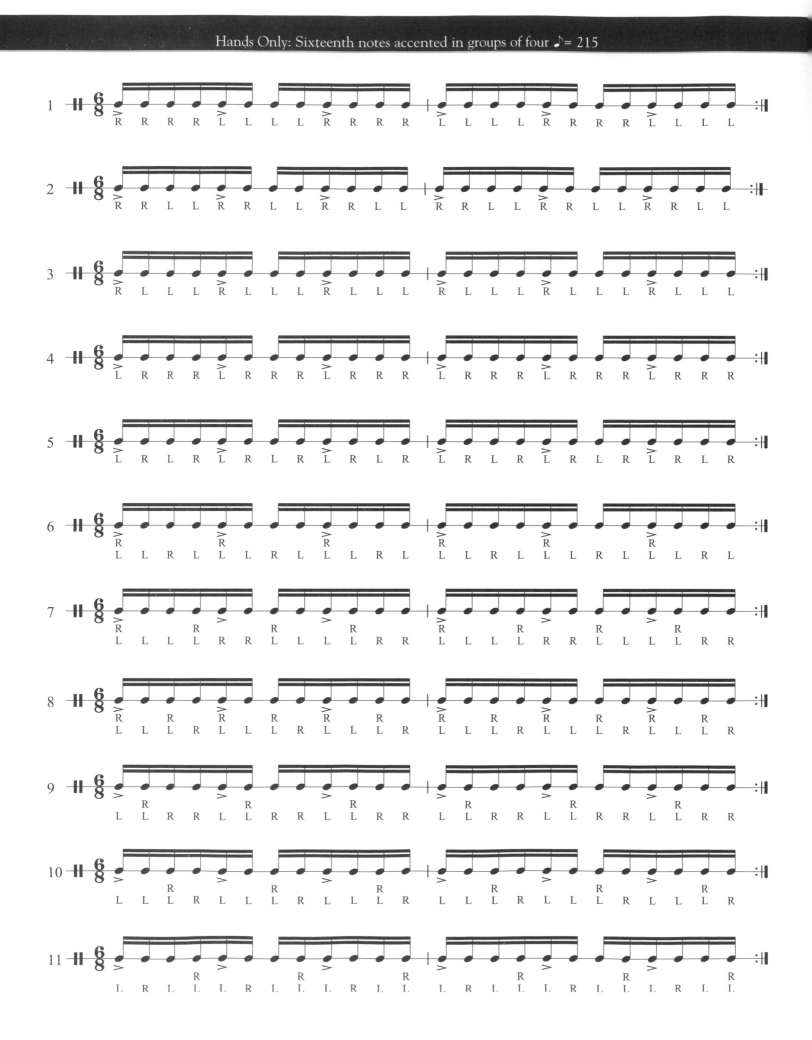

Hands Only: Sixteenth notes accented in groups of five ♪= 215

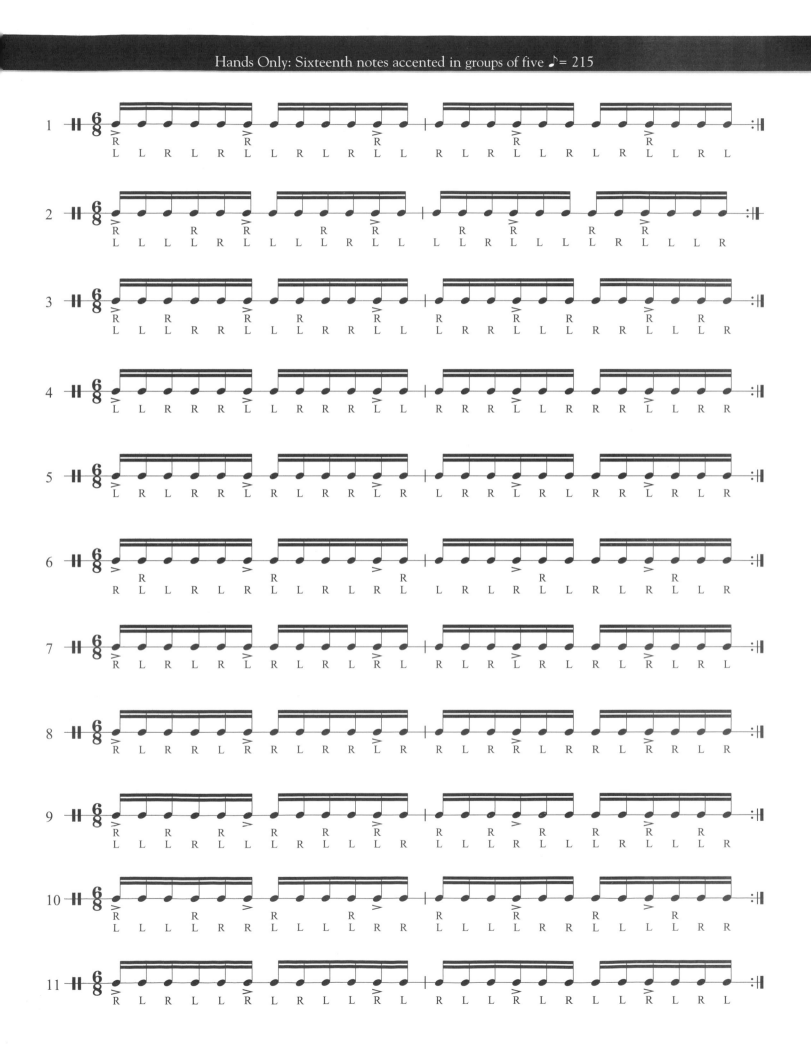

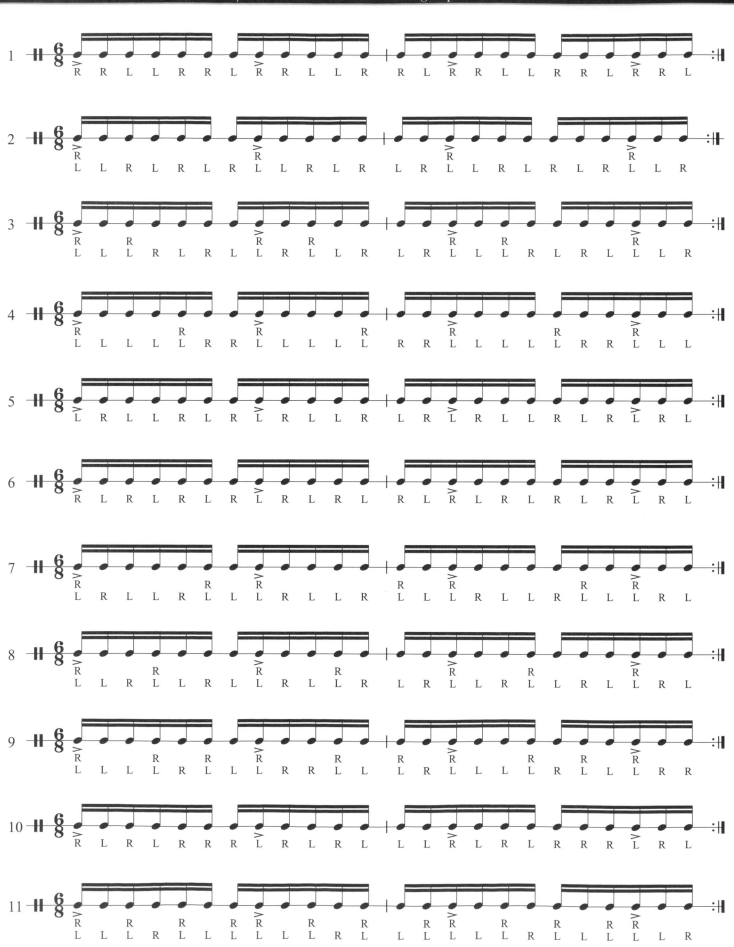

Six–Eight Song

Grooves

Regular rhythm

This is what a typical six–eight pattern looks like:

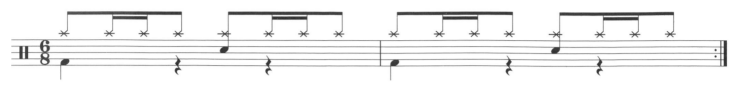

Now let's review different variations.

Groove 1

Practice CD	Track 41	
Performance CD	Track 3	Time :34

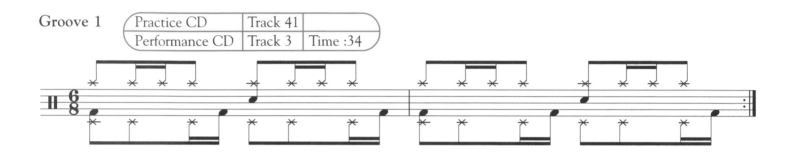

Groove 2

Practice CD	Track 42	
Performance CD	Track 3	Time :48

Groove 3

Practice CD	Track 43	
Performance CD	Track 3	Time 1:01

Groove 4

Practice CD	Track 43	
Performance CD	Track 3	Time 1:14

Fills

Each of the exercises in this book has a length of four bars. However, note that it would take three bars for each grouping of Threes to complete a cycle (so that the beginning of the grouping lands back on beat one). It would take Fours four bars to complete a cycle (which is how they are written throughout the book). Fives would complete its cycle in five bars, and Sevens would cycle in seven bars. For the sake of musicality and continuity throughout this book, each exercise is limited to four bars. Therefore, with the exception of the Fours segments, the final grouping at the end of the fourth bar is cut short.

Groups of Threes

Fill 1

Practice CD	Track 45	
Performance CD	Track 3	Time :41

Fill 2

Practice CD	Track 45	
Performance CD	Track 3	Time :54

Fill 3

Practice CD	Track 45	
Performance CD	Track 3	Time 1:08

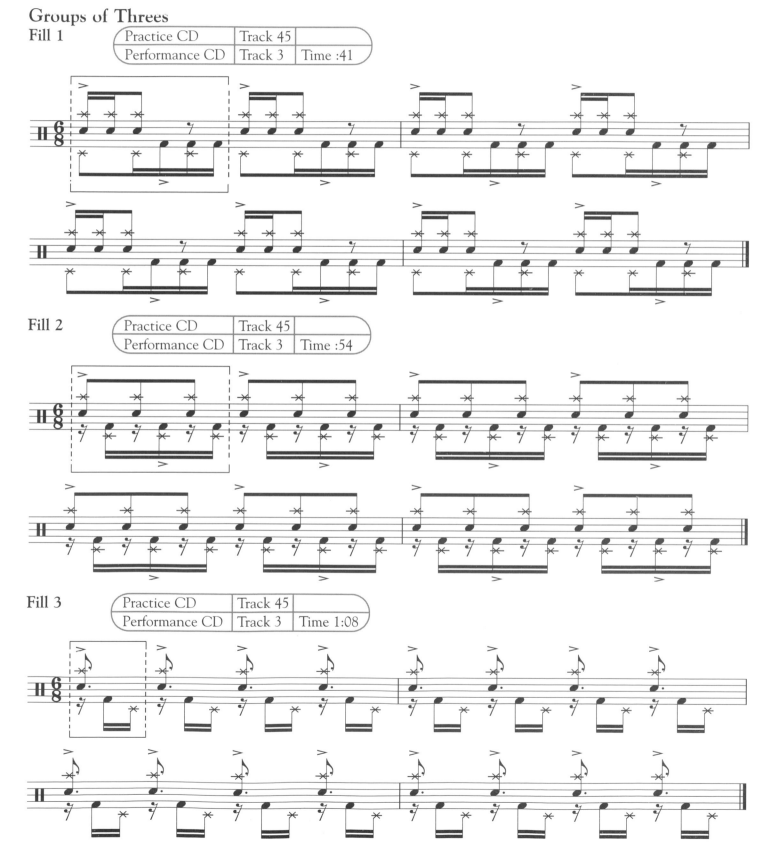

Check out *Fill 4* on track 46 of the practice CD. The grouping is accented every third note instead of on the downbeats as written. Displacing the grouped accents like this adds variety. Try this approach with all the exercises throughout the book.

Fill 4

Practice CD	Track 46	
Performance CD	Track 3	Time 1:21

Fill 5

Practice CD	Track 46	
Performance CD	Track 3	Time 1:34

Fill 6

Practice CD	Track 46	
Performance CD	Track 3	Time 1:48

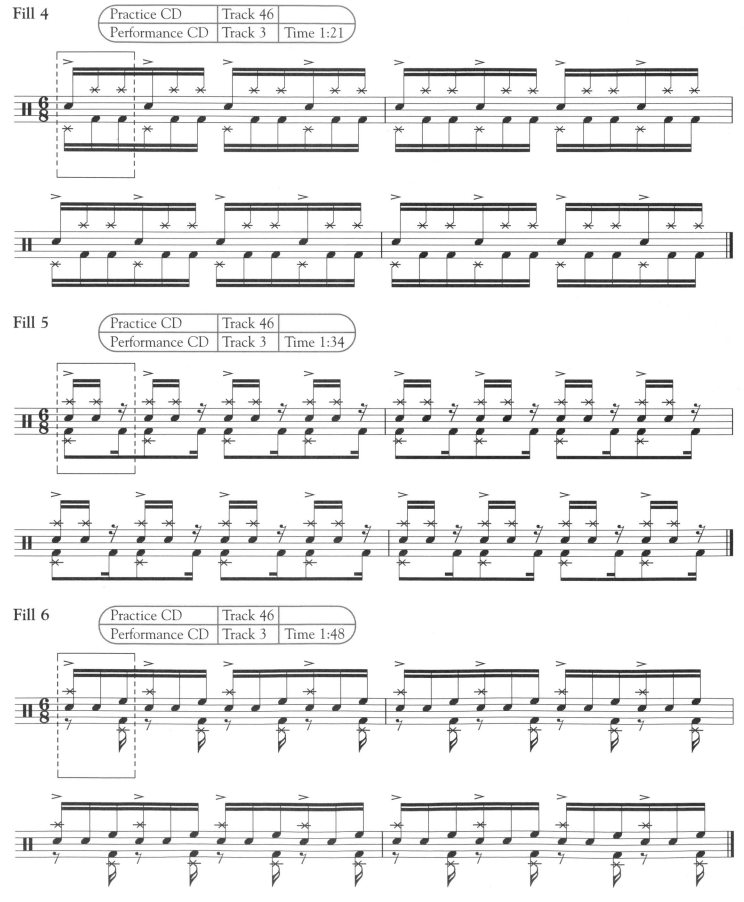

Fill 7

Practice CD	Track 47	
Performance CD	Track 3	Time 2:01

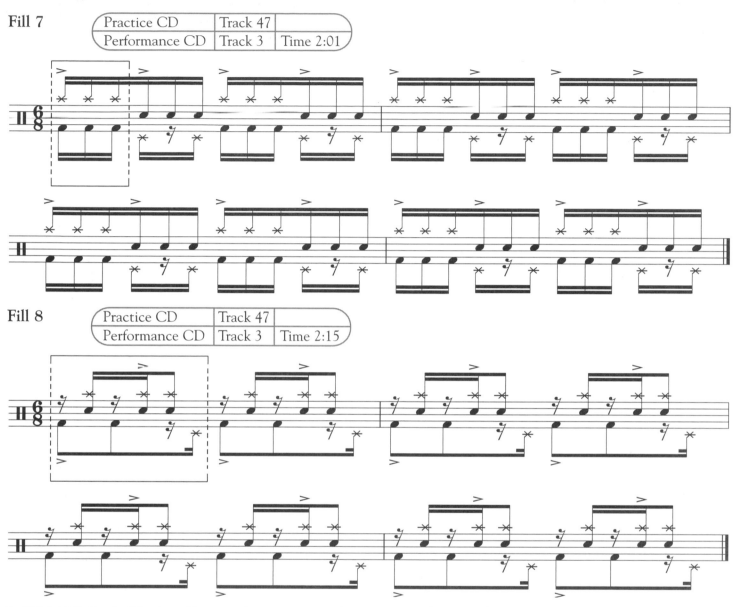

Fill 8

Practice CD	Track 47	
Performance CD	Track 3	Time 2:15

In *Fill 9* (CD Track 47), the offbeat crashes are accented instead of the downbeats as written. Displacing the grouped accents like this adds variety. Try this approach with all the exercises throughout the book.

Fill 9

Practice CD	Track 47	
Performance CD	Track 3	Time 2:28

Fill 10

Practice CD	Track 48	
Performance CD	Track 3	Time 2:41

Fill 11

Practice CD	Track 48	
Performance CD	Track 3	Time 2:55

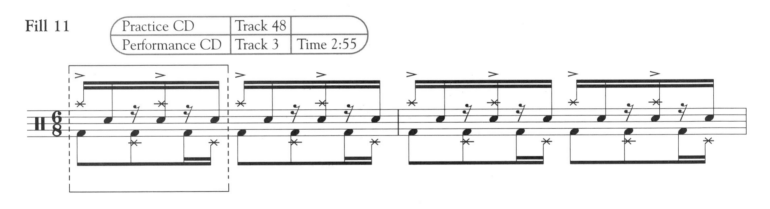

Groups of Fours

Fill 1

| Practice CD | Track 49 | |
| Performance CD | Track 3 | Time 3:08 |

Fill 2

| Practice CD | Track 49 | |
| Performance CD | Track 3 | Time 3:21 |

Fill 3

| Practice CD | Track 49 | |
| Performance CD | Track 3 | Time 3:35 |

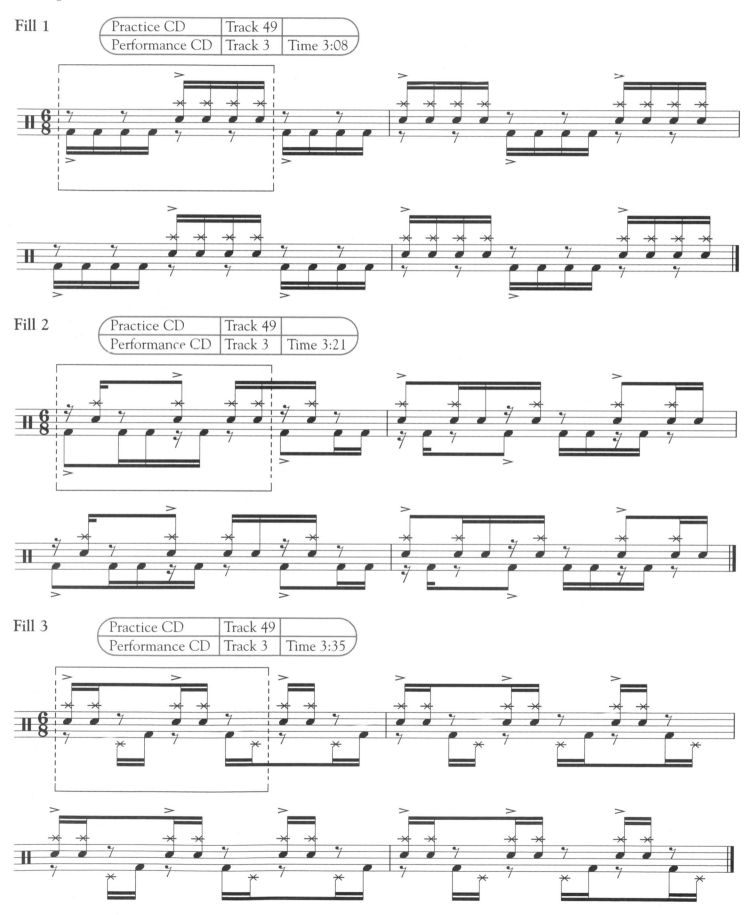

Fill 4

| Practice CD | Track 50 | |
| Performance CD | Track 3 | Time 3:48 |

Fill 5

| Practice CD | Track 50 | |
| Performance CD | Track 3 | Time 4:02 |

Fill 6

| Practice CD | Track 50 | |
| Performance CD | Track 3 | Time 4:15 |

Fill 7

| Practice CD | Track 51 | |
| Performance CD | Track 3 | Time 4:28 |

Fill 8

| Practice CD | Track 51 | |
| Performance CD | Track 3 | Time 4:42 |

Fill 9

| Practice CD | Track 51 | |
| Performance CD | Track 3 | Time 4:55 |

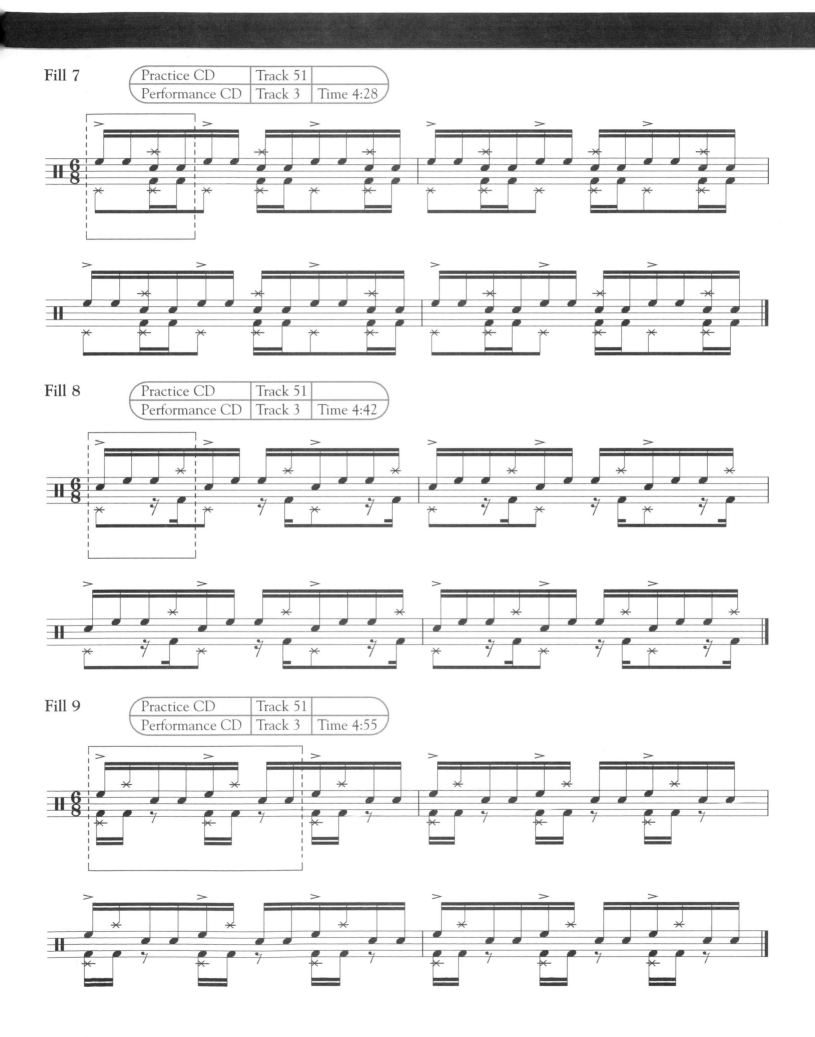

Fill 10

Practice CD	Track 52	
Performance CD	Track 3	Time 5:09

Fill 11

Practice CD	Track 52	
Performance CD	Track 3	Time 5:22

Groups of Fives

Notice how in *Fill 1* on CD track 53, every ten notes are emphasized instead of every five notes.

Fill 1

Practice CD	Track 53	
Performance CD	Track 3	Time 5:35

Fill 2

Practice CD	Track 53	
Performance CD	Track 3	Time 5:49

Fill 3

Practice CD	Track 53	
Performance CD	Track 3	Time 6:02

Fill 4

Practice CD	Track 54	
Performance CD	Track 3	Time 6:16

Fill 5

Practice CD	Track 54	
Performance CD	Track 3	Time 6:29

Fill 6

Practice CD	Track 54	
Performance CD	Track 3	Time 6:42

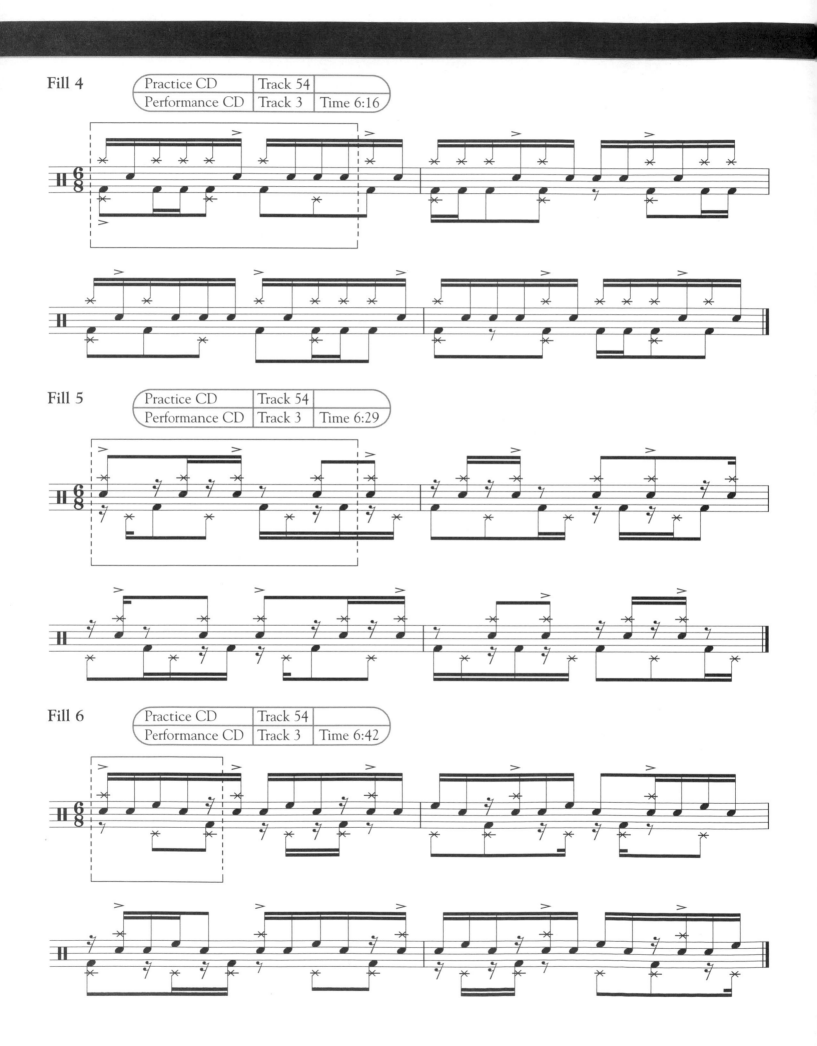

Fill 7

Practice CD	Track 55	
Performance CD	Track 3	Time 6:56

Fill 8

Practice CD	Track 55	
Performance CD	Track 3	7:09

Fill 9

Practice CD	Track 55	
Performance CD	Track 3	Time 7:23

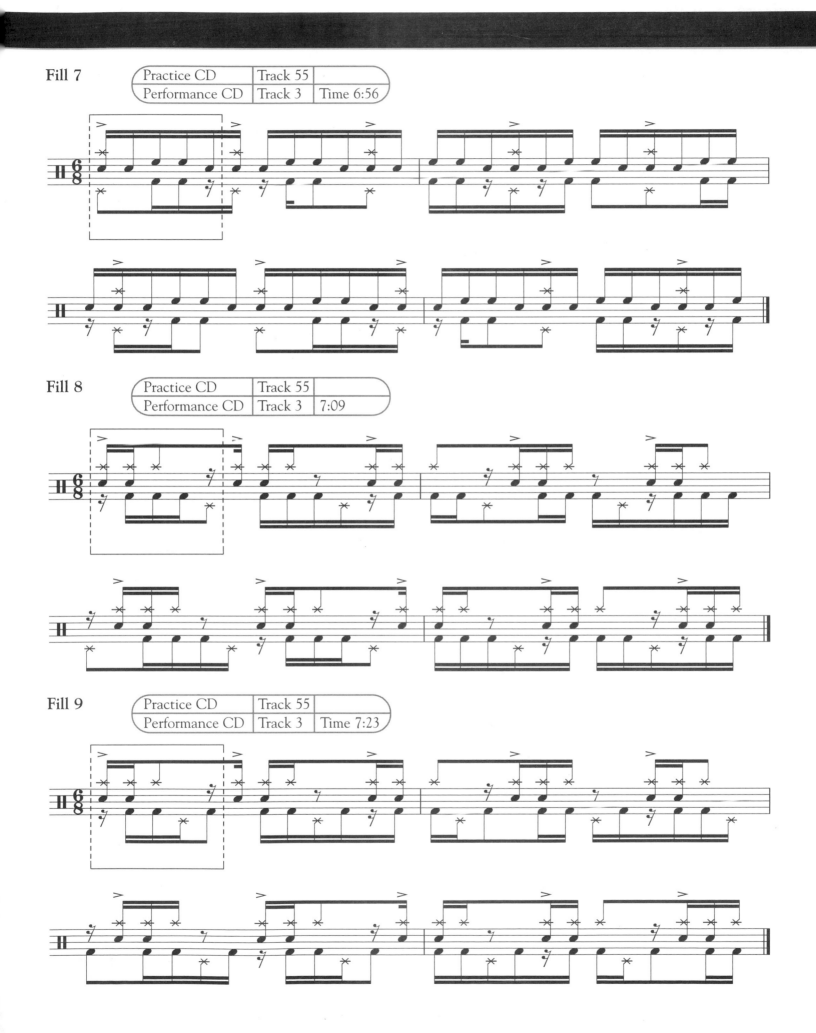

Fill 10

Practice CD	Track 56	
Performance CD	Track 3	Time 7:36

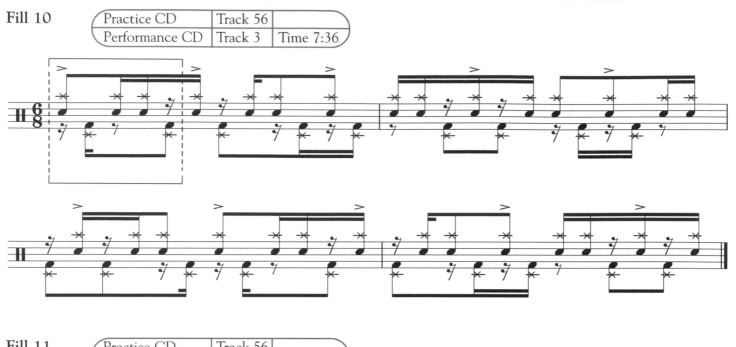

Fill 11

Practice CD	Track 56	
Performance CD	Track 3	Time 7:49

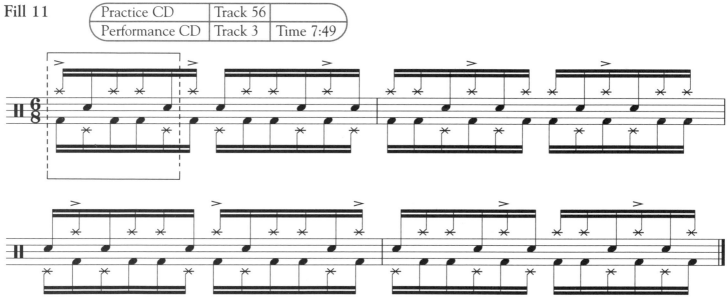

Groups of Sevens

Fill 1

Practice CD	Track 57	
Performance CD	Track 3	Time 8:03

Fill 2

Practice CD	Track 57	
Performance CD	Track 3	Time 8:16

Fill 3

Practice CD	Track 57	
Performance CD	Track 3	Time 8:29

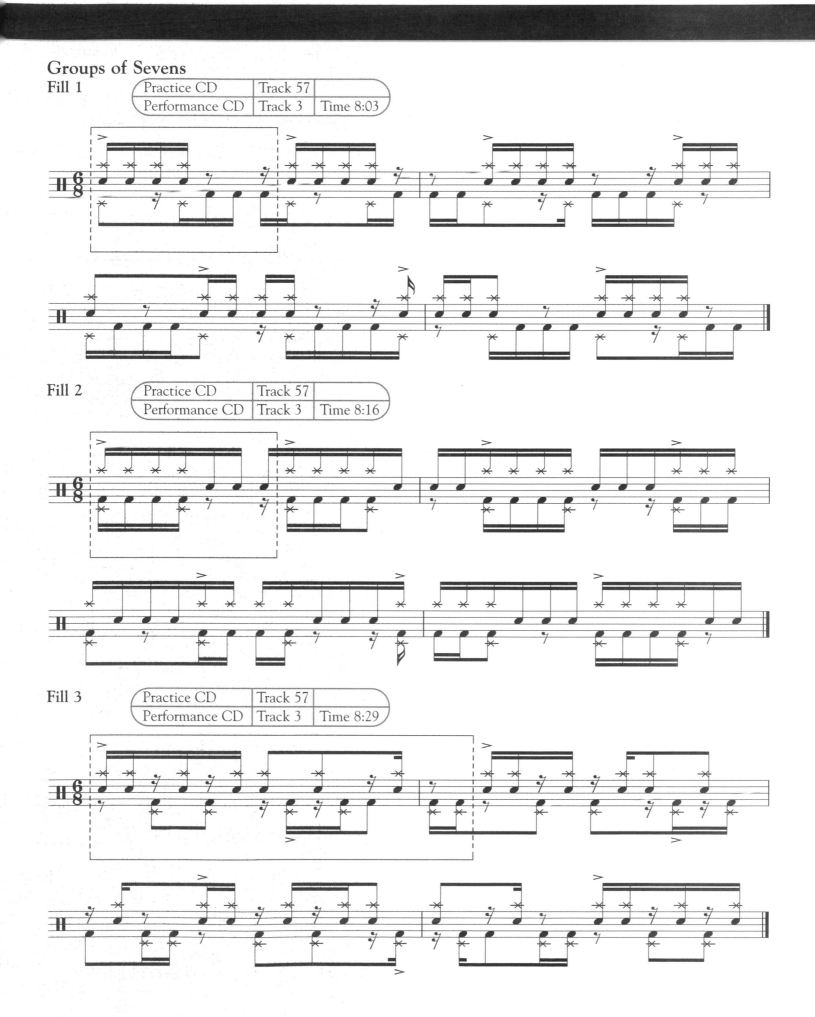

Fill 4

Practice CD	Track 58	
Performance CD	Track 3	Time 8:43

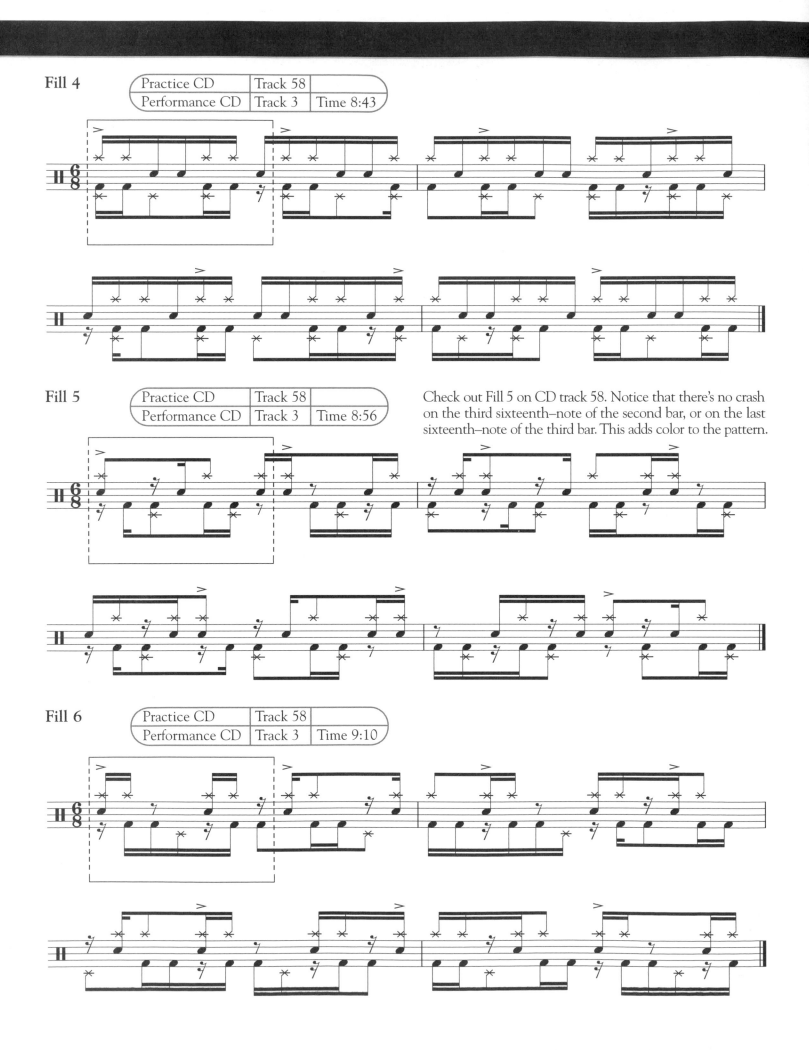

Fill 5

Practice CD	Track 58	
Performance CD	Track 3	Time 8:56

Check out Fill 5 on CD track 58. Notice that there's no crash on the third sixteenth–note of the second bar, or on the last sixteenth–note of the third bar. This adds color to the pattern.

Fill 6

Practice CD	Track 58	
Performance CD	Track 3	Time 9:10

Fill 7

| Practice CD | Track 59 | |
| Performance CD | Track 3 | Time 9:23 |

Fill 8

| Practice CD | Track 59 | |
| Performance CD | Track 3 | Time 9:37 |

Fill 9

| Practice CD | Track 59 | |
| Performance CD | Track 3 | Time 9:50 |

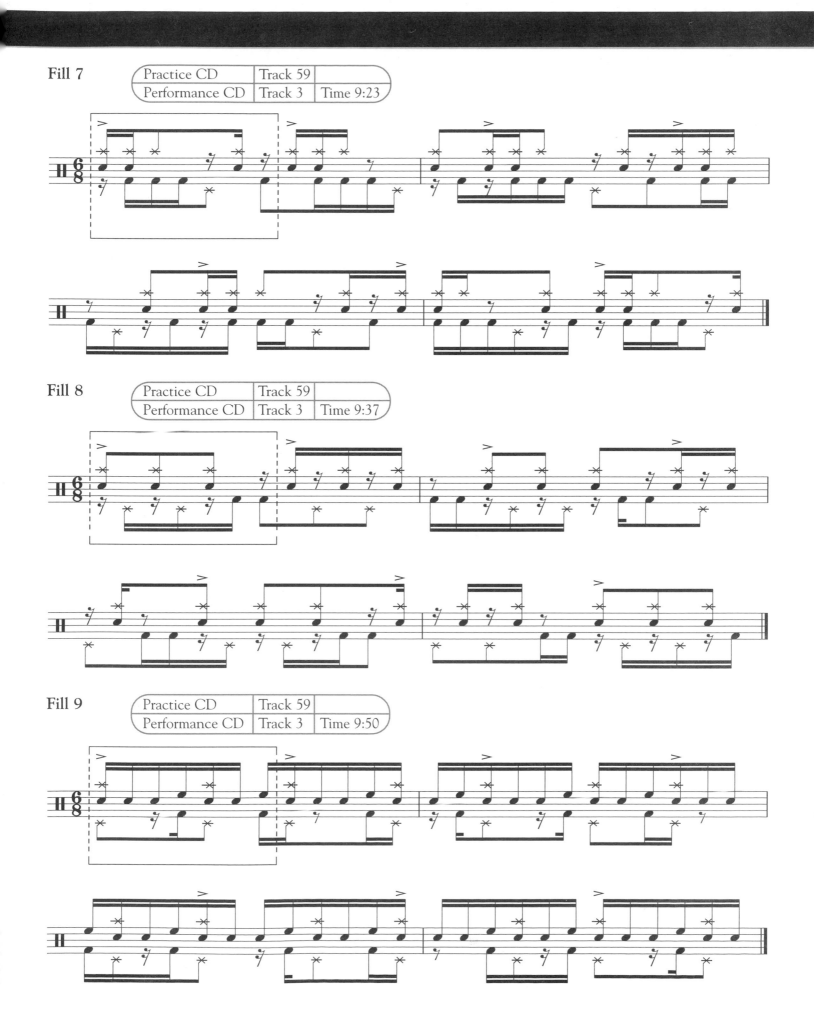

Fill 10

Practice CD	Track 60	
Performance CD	Track 3	Time 10:03

Fill 11

Practice CD	Track 60	
Performance CD	Track 3	Time 10:17

Chapter 4: Funk

Four–bar funk grooves alternating with four bar
sixteenth–note triplet exercises accented in
groups of threes, fours, fives, and sevens.

Hands Only: Sixteenth–note triplets accented in groups of three ♩= 87

Hands Only: Sixteenth–note triplets accented in groups of four ♩= 87

Hands Only: Sixteenth–note triplets accented in groups of five ♩= 87

Hands Only: Sixteenth–note triplets accented in groups of seven ♩= 87

Funk Song

Fine

Grooves

Regular rhythm

This is what a typical funk pattern looks like:

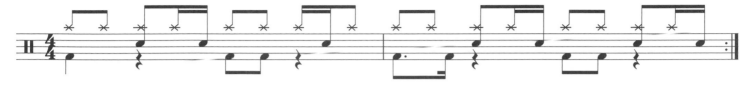

Now let's review different variations.

In this chapter, the drumset exercises accented in groups of threes are actually written as groups of sixes. They are labeled as "threes" to keep consistent with the rest of the book, but in actual playing they go by so fast that it's generally more musical to accent these patterns in six–note groupings.

Groove 1

| Practice CD | Track 61 | |
| Performance CD | Track 4 | Time 0:35 |

Check out Groove 1 on track 61 of the practice CD. There's an additional bass drum note on the "e" of beat four in the second bar. This adds variety to the groove.

Groove 2

| Practice CD | Track 62 | |
| Performance CD | Track 4 | Time 1:07 |

Groove 3

| Practice CD | Track 63 | |
| Performance CD | Track 4 | Time 1:29 |

Listen to track 63 and pay close attention to the notation. The hi–hat pattern is played with the right hand, not the left foot as in most of this book.

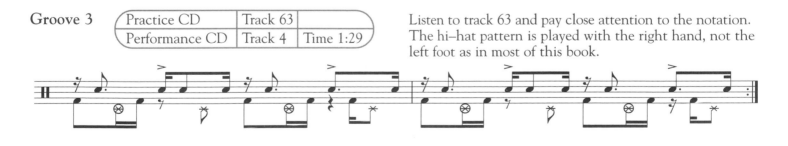

Groove 4

| Practice CD | Track 64 | |
| Performance CD | Track 4 | Time 1:51 |

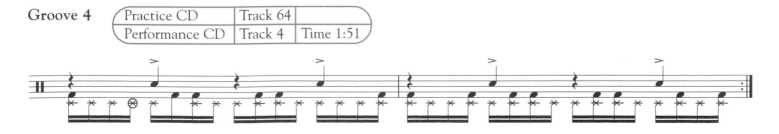

Fills

Groups of Threes

Fill 1

Practice CD	Track 65	
Performance CD	Track 4	Time 0:55

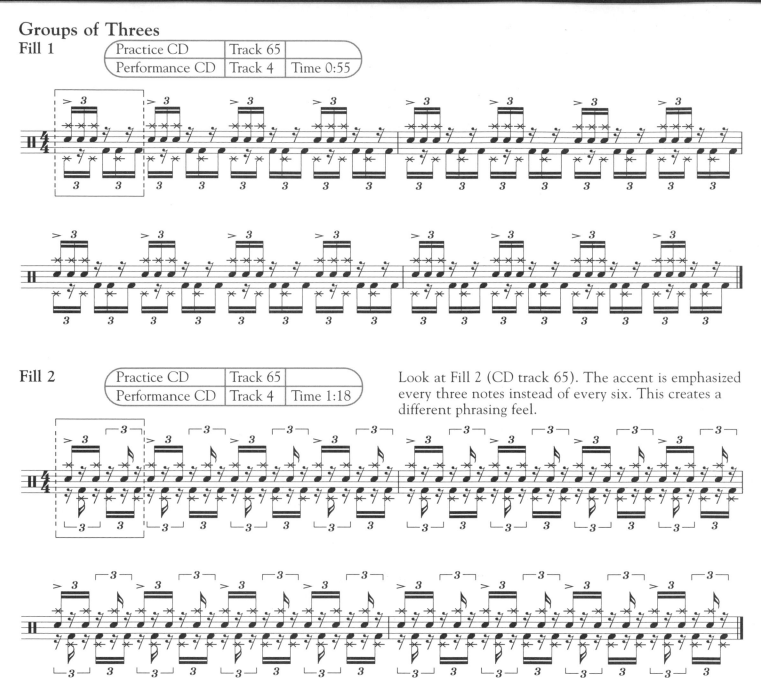

Fill 2

Practice CD	Track 65	
Performance CD	Track 4	Time 1:18

Look at Fill 2 (CD track 65). The accent is emphasized every three notes instead of every six. This creates a different phrasing feel.

Fill 3

Practice CD	Track 65	
Performance CD	Track 4	Time 1:40

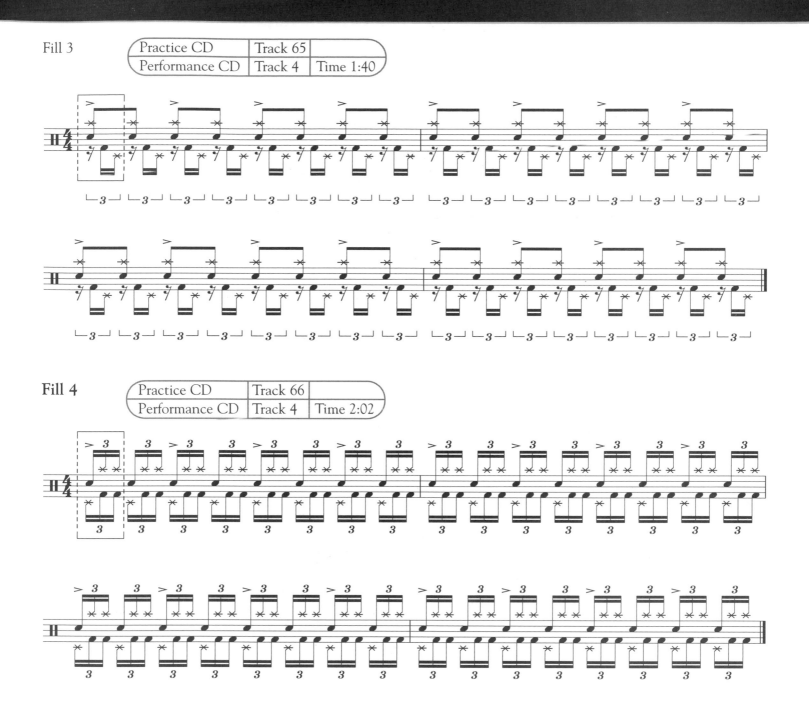

Fill 4

Practice CD	Track 66	
Performance CD	Track 4	Time 2:02

Fill 5

Practice CD	Track 66	
Performance CD	Track 4	Time 2:24

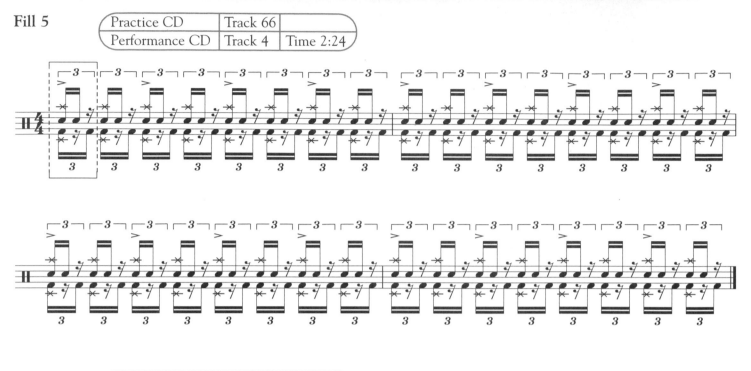

Fill 6

Practice CD	Track 66	
Performance CD	Track 4	Time 2:46

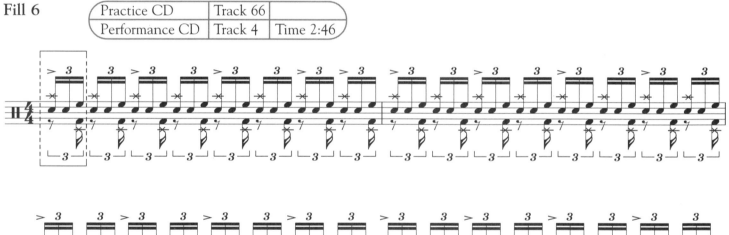

Fill 7

Practice CD	Track 67	
Performance CD	Track 4	Time 3:09

Fill 8

Practice CD	Track 67	
Performance CD	Track 4	Time 3:31

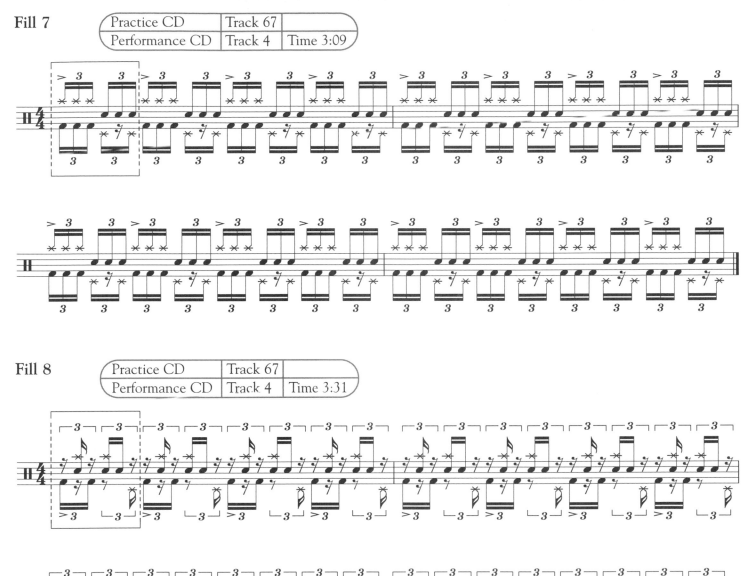

Fill 9

| Practice CD | Track 67 | |
| Performance CD | Track 4 | Time 3:53 |

Fill 10

| Practice CD | Track 68 | |
| Performance CD | Track 4 | Time 4:15 |

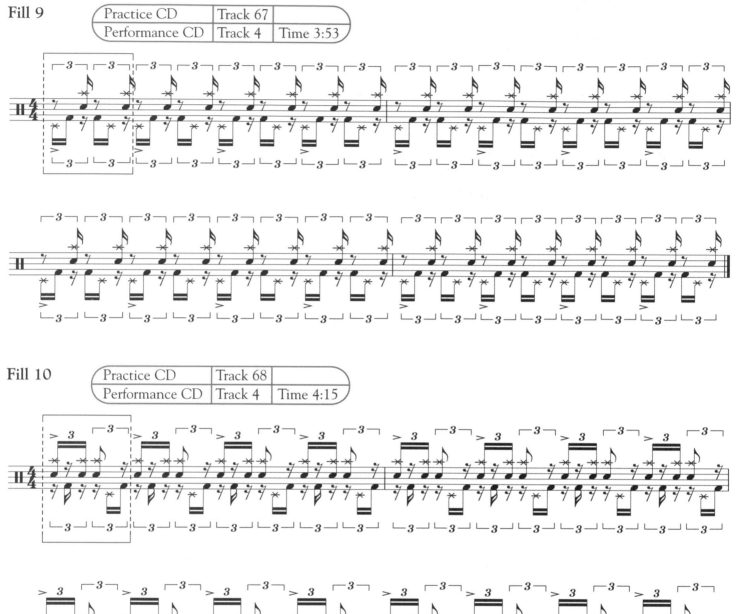

Fill 11

Practice CD	Track 68	
Performance CD	Track 4	Time 4:37

In *Fill 11* (CD track 68), the accent is emphasized every three notes instead of every six. This adds a variation on the phrasing.

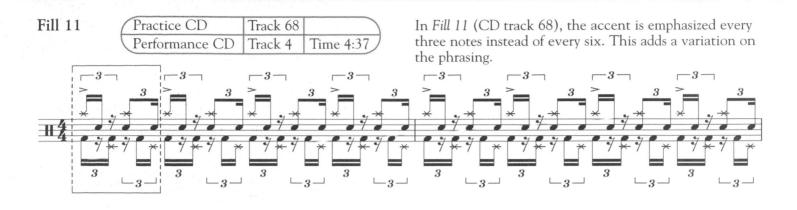

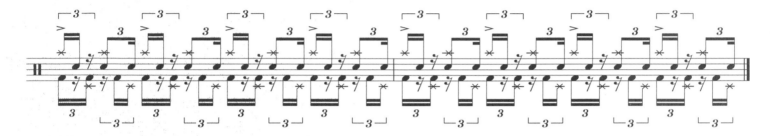

Groups of Fours

Fill 1

Practice CD	Track 69	
Performance CD	Track 4	Time 4:59

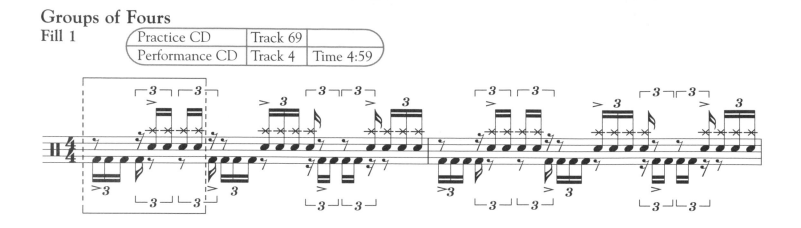

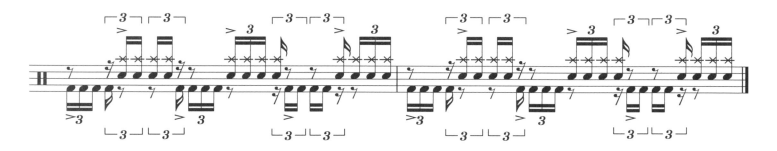

Fill 2

Practice CD	Track 69	
Performance CD	Track 4	Time 5:21

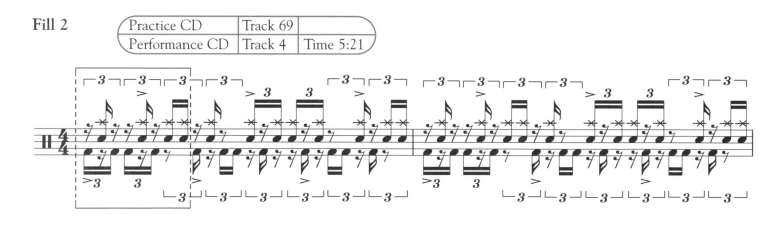

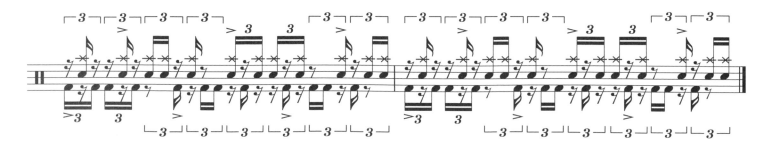

Fill 3

Practice CD	Track 69	
Performance CD	Track 4	Time 5:43

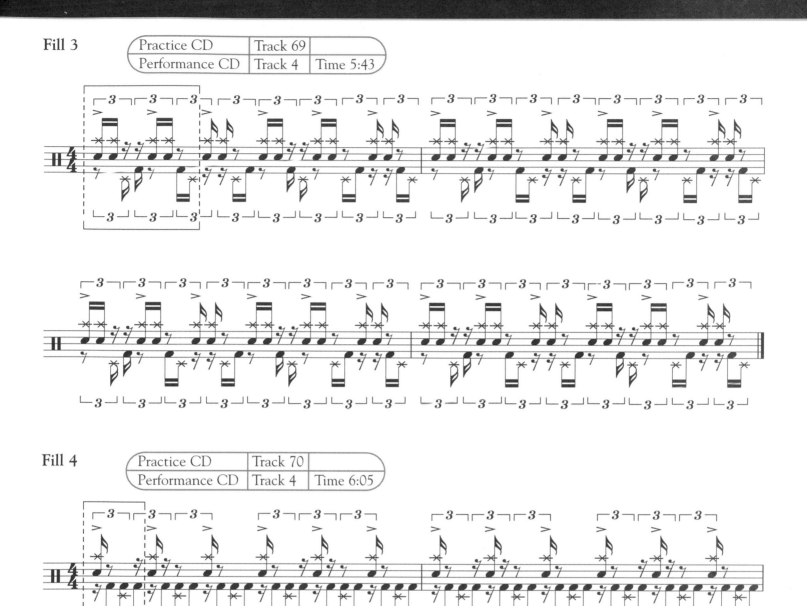

Fill 4

Practice CD	Track 70	
Performance CD	Track 4	Time 6:05

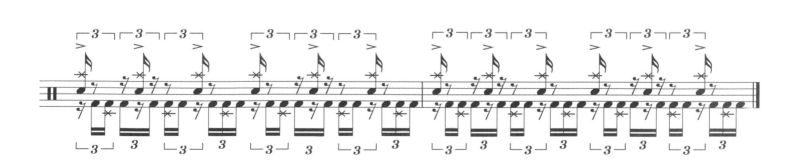

Fill 5

| Practice CD | Track 70 | |
| Performance CD | Track 4 | Time 6:27 |

Fill 6

| Practice CD | Track 70 | |
| Performance CD | Track 4 | Time 6:49 |

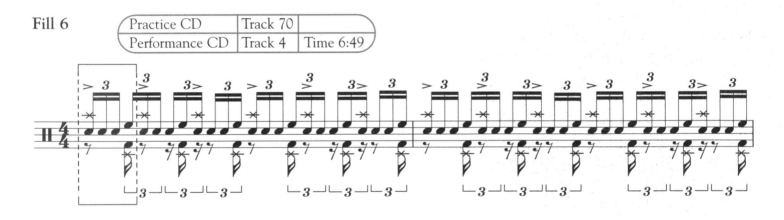
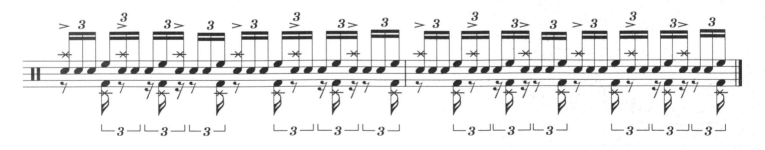

Fill 7

Practice CD	Track 71	
Performance CD	Track 4	Time 7:11

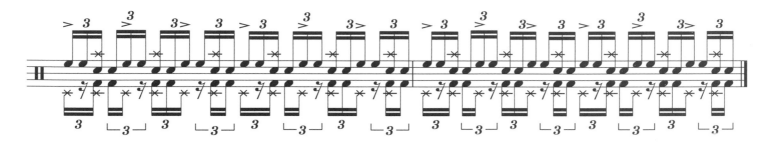

Fill 8

Practice CD	Track 71	
Performance CD	Track 4	Time 7:33

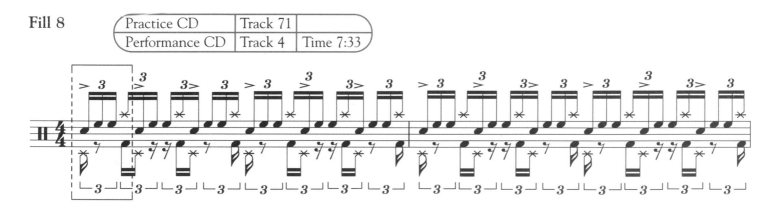

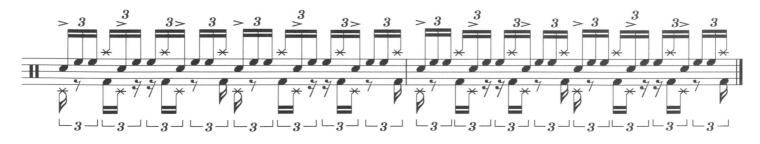

Fill 9

Practice CD	Track 71	
Performance CD	Track 4	Time 7:55

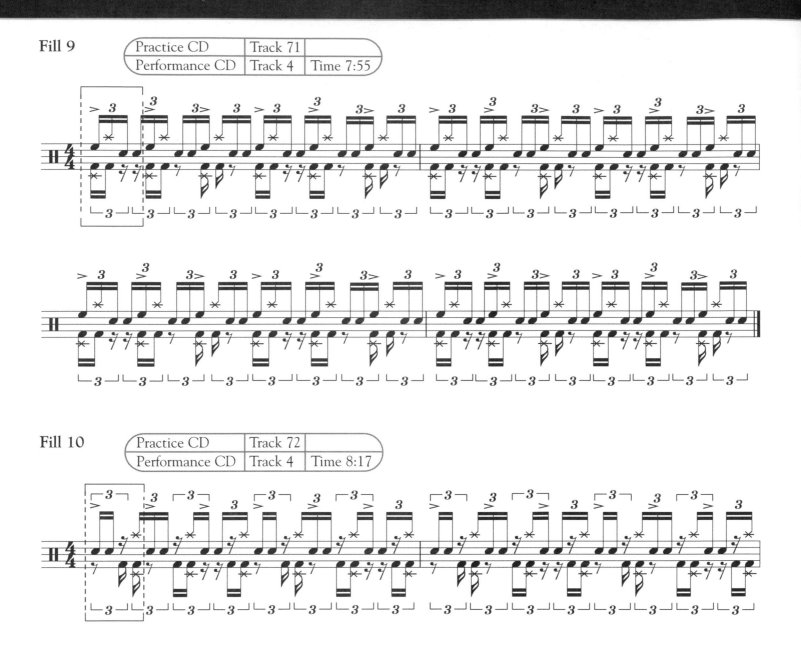

Fill 10

Practice CD	Track 72	
Performance CD	Track 4	Time 8:17

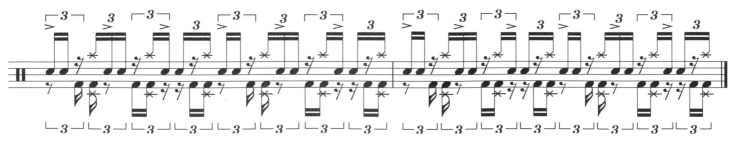

Fill 11

Practice CD	Track 72	
Performance CD	Track 4	Time 8:40

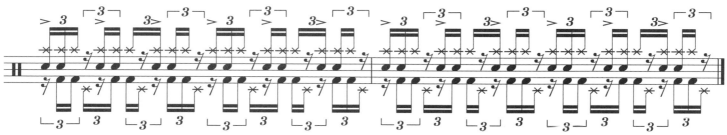

Groups of Fives

Fill 1

Practice CD	Track 73	
Performance CD	Track 4	Time 9:02

In *Fill 1* (CD track 73), the emphasis falls every ten notes instead of every five. Try placing the accents in different places to create new and interesting musical phrases.

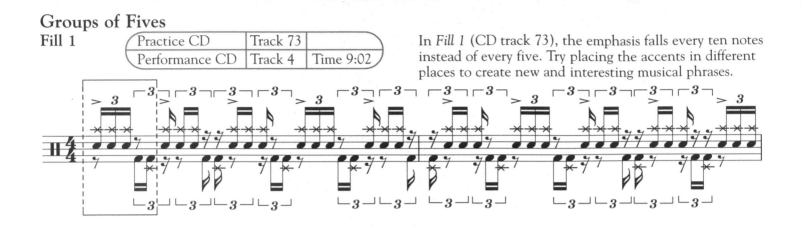

Fill 2

Practice CD	Track 73	
Performance CD	Track 4	Time 9:24

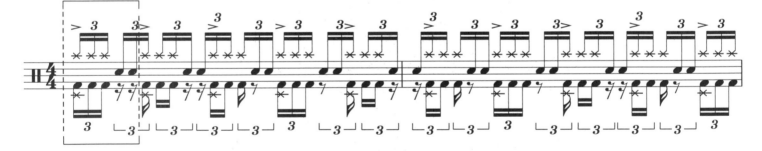

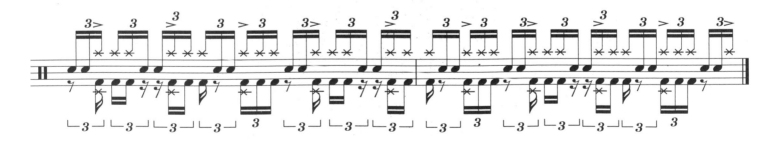

Fill 3

| Practice CD | Track 73 | |
| Performance CD | Track 4 | Time 9:46 |

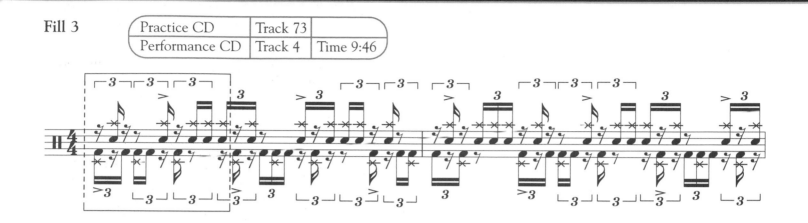

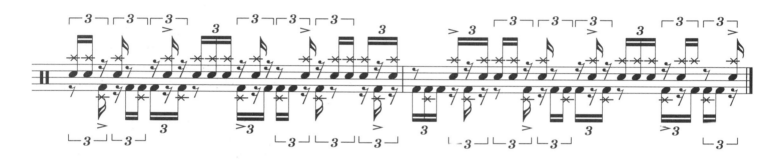

Fill 4

| Practice CD | Track 74 | |
| Performance CD | Track 4 | Time 10:08 |

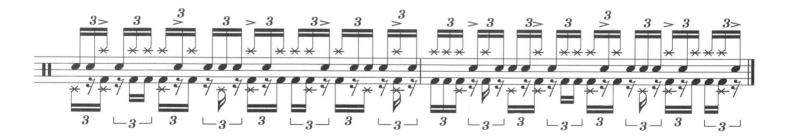

Fill 5

Practice CD	Track 74	
Performance CD	Track 4	Time 10:30

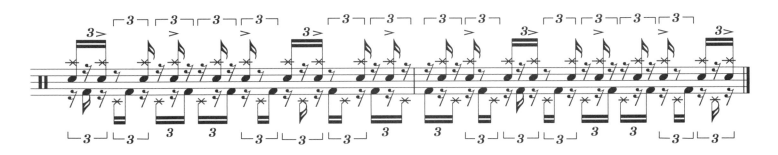

Fill 6

Practice CD	Track 74	
Performance CD	Track 4	Time 10:52

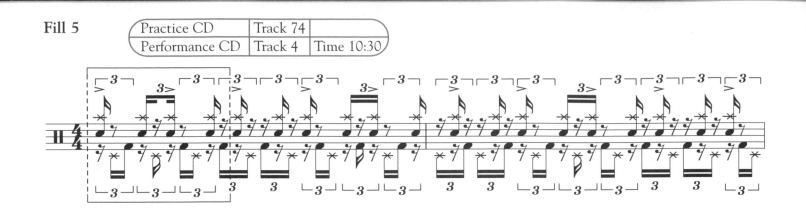

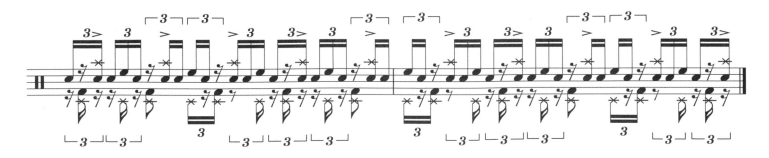

Fill 7

Practice CD	Track 75	
Performance CD	Track 4	Time 11:14

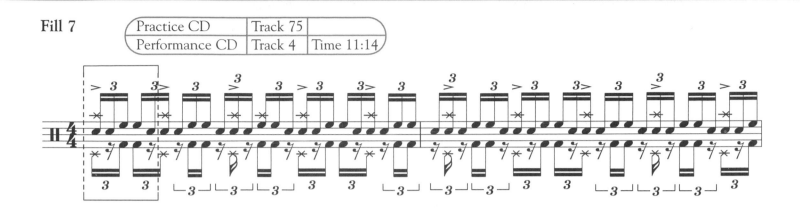

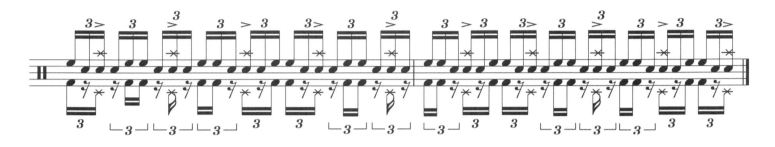

Fill 8

Practice CD	Track 75	
Performance CD	Track 4	Time 11:36

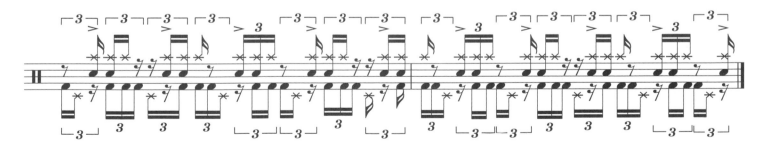

Fill 9

Practice CD	Track 75	
Performance CD	Track 4	Time 11:58

Fill 10

Practice CD	Track 76	
Performance CD	Track 4	Time 12:20

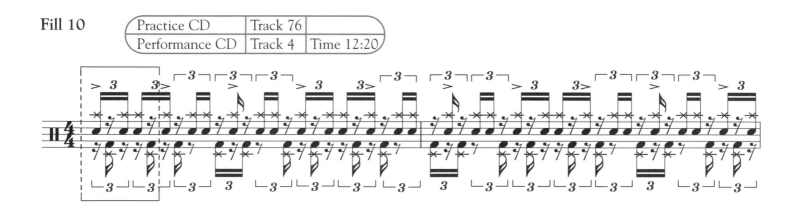

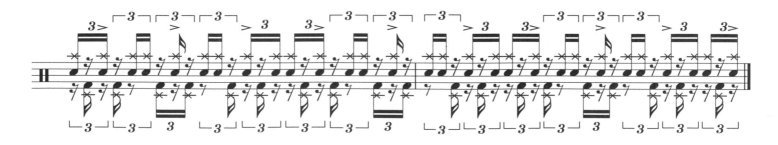

Fill 11

Practice CD	Track 76	
Performance CD	Track 4	Time 12:42

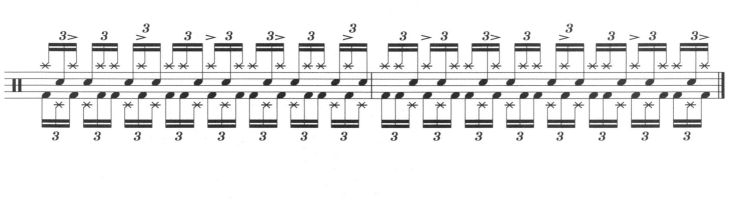

Groups of Sevens

Fill 1

Practice CD	Track 77	
Performance CD	Track 4	Time 13:04

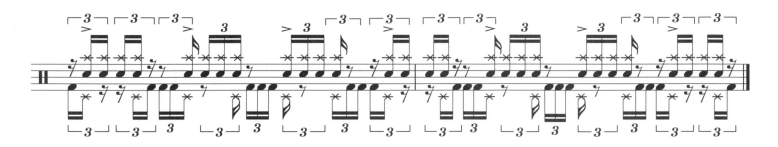

Fill 2

Practice CD	Track 77	
Performance CD	Track 4	Time 13:26

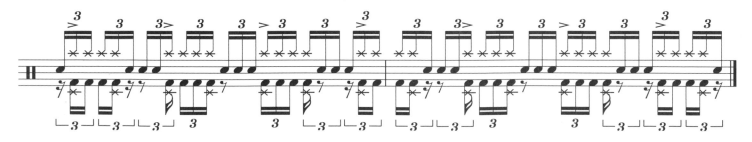

Fill 3

Practice CD	Track 77	
Performance CD	Track 4	Time 13:48

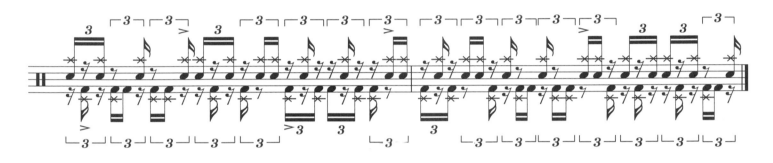

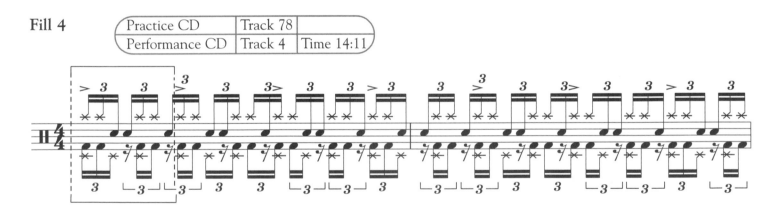

Fill 4

Practice CD	Track 78	
Performance CD	Track 4	Time 14:11

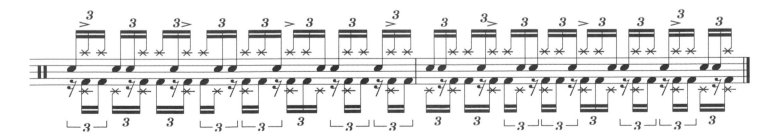

Fill 5

| Practice CD | Track 78 | |
| Performance CD | Track 4 | Time 14:33 |

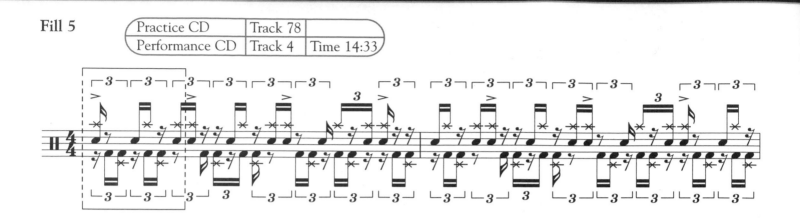

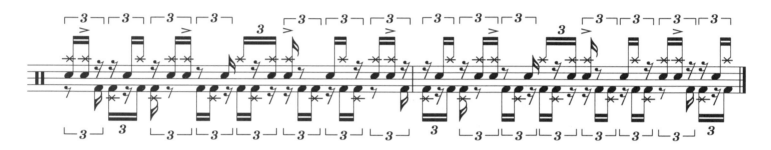

Fill 6

| Practice CD | Track 78 | |
| Performance CD | Track 4 | Time 14:55 |

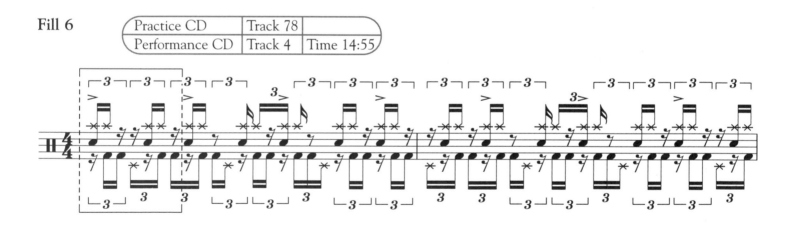

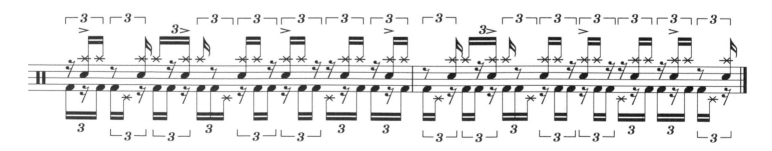

Fill 7

Practice CD	Track 79	
Performance CD	Track 4	Time 15:17

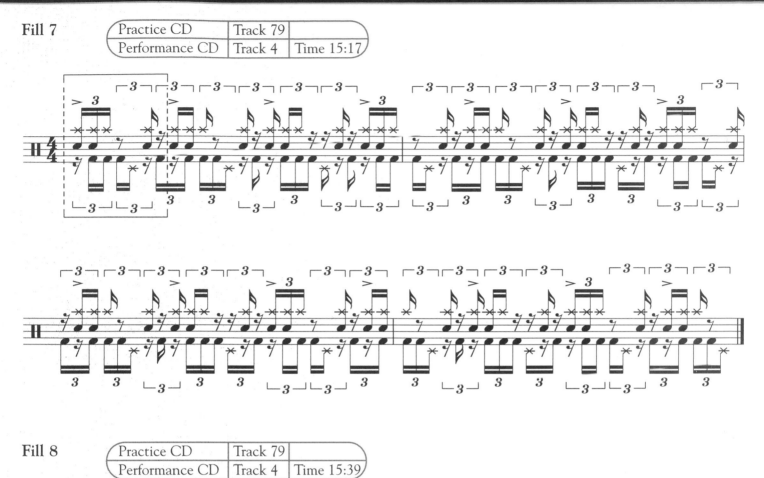

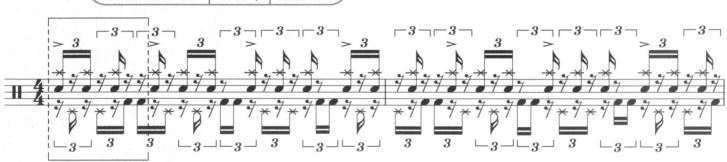

Fill 8

Practice CD	Track 79	
Performance CD	Track 4	Time 15:39

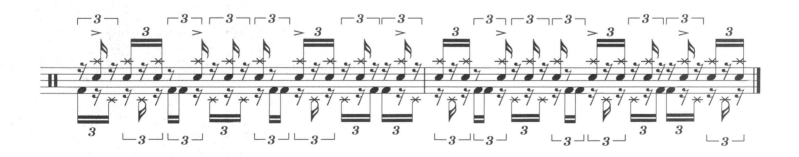

Fill 9

| Practice CD | Track 79 | |
| Performance CD | Track 4 | Time 16:01 |

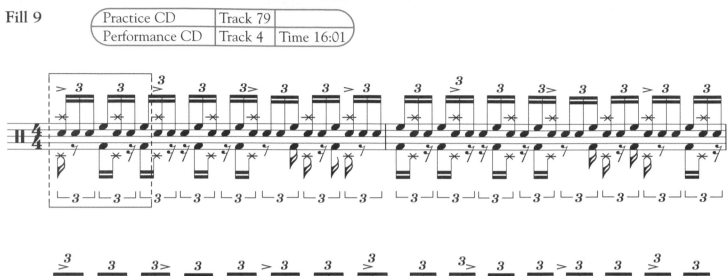

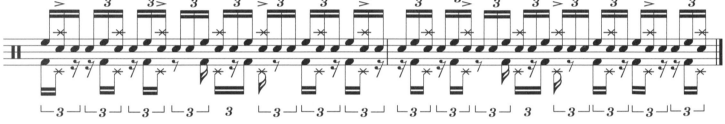

Fill 10

| Practice CD | Track 80 | |
| Performance CD | Track 4 | Time 16:23 |

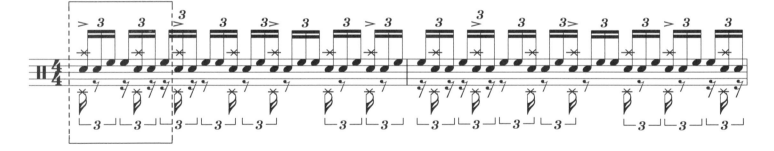

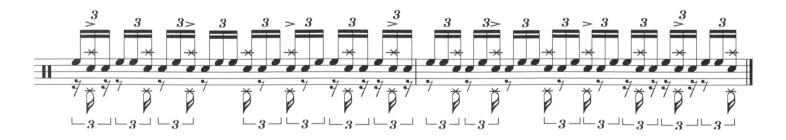

Fill 11

Practice CD	Track 80	
Performance CD	Track 4	Time 16:45

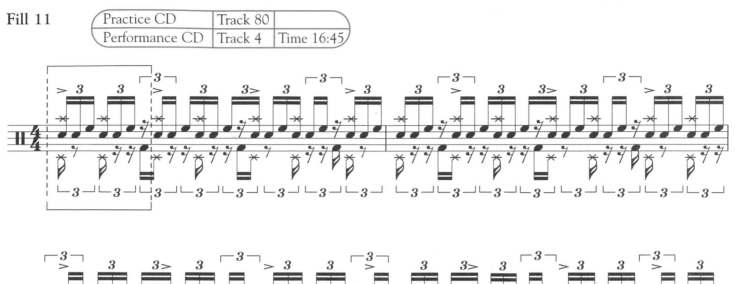

Terry Silverlight

Terry Silverlight has been involved with many facets of the music business, contributing his musical talents as a leader, drummer, composer, producer, arranger, author and educator to projects in almost every style of music.

Terry has performed all over the world and has played drums on gold and platinum recordings for George Benson, Natalie Merchant, Freddie Jackson, Stephanie Mills, Tom Jones, Laura Nyro, Anne Murray, Mel Torme, Jennifer Holladay, Phil Woods, The Fania All–Stars, The CTI All–Stars, Jonathan Butler, movie scores for One Fine Day, You've Got Mail, Object Of My Affection, Titus, Frida, Slaves Of New York, What Planet Are You From and countless jingles and TV shows. Terry has toured extensively with artists such as Roberta Flack and the award–winning, all–star Manhattan Jazz Orchestra.

Terry has written, produced and arranged hundreds of pieces for network TV shows including: One Life To Live, The Sopranos, All My Children, Ed, Beverly Hills 90210, Young And The Restless, Melrose Place; jingles for Reebok, Nicorette, Pantene, Crisco Canola, songs in the films Marci X, Mad About Mambo, Head Over Heels, etc. His songs have been recorded by Nancy Wilson, Carl Anderson, Les McCann, Louise (top ten single in the UK) and Philip Ingram.

Terry Silverlight endorses: Gretsch, ProMark, Paiste and Evans.

Terry has released two solo artist CDs: *Terry Silverlight* and the brand new *Wild!!*

For more information, visit: www.terrysilverlight.com.